3rd GRADE
MATH
ADVENTURES

FUN LEARNING

=

*

3rd Grade Math Adventures

Copyright© 2023 Amit Uppal

CONTENTS

FOR PARENTS

As a father of a 9-year-old, I learned and quickly realized that the best way for kids to learn math is not through boring exercises but through fun, interesting stories, and puzzles.

Engaging kids in fun activities and stories that involve math can help them develop a positive attitude towards the subject, making it less intimidating and more enjoyable. When children are enjoying themselves and feel like they are playing, they are more likely to learn and retain the information being taught. The goal of this book is to provide a platform for kids where they can learn through questions that interest them, make them laugh, make them think and in the process help them learn. I really hope that this book will help kids learn math in a fun and engaging way.

HOW TO GRADE EACH EXERCISE

This book is divided into number of chapters. Each chapter contains missions. Your goal is to complete these missions. For each mission you complete, you earn a badge. Your goal is to collect 13 badges. All badges are on the last two pages of the book. As you earn them, put a checkmark in front of each badge.

Answers to missions are provided at the end of each chapter. The number of questions in each mission can vary. For example, if there are 10 questions in the mission and you answer 8 questions correctly, then you get 8 out of 10. When you grade yourself, you can write 8 in the top section of the circle, like the example below. Good luck!

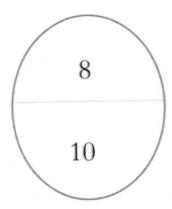

CHAPTER 1

Addition

Introduction

We learned about addition in the second grade. In this chapter, we are going to meet our new friend, Spooky, first, then practice addition, and finally, go on a mission to help Spooky. Hope you all are ready for some fun!

Join Spooky on a Math Adventure to Get His Dream Waterslide!

Before we start learning addition, I want all of you to meet "Spooky". Spooky wants his dad to buy a big waterslide for him so that he can have a lot of fun in his backyard.

Spooky is very much like us, except he walks upside down at home. When he was eight years old, Spooky used to be very good at math. However, when he turned nine, he got distracted and stopped learning math, losing his focus. His dad tried to teach him, but Spooky was not interested. To bring his interest back, his dad came up with what he thought was a brilliant idea - he gave Spooky a mission. He told Spooky, "I will ask you a few math questions; if you have more right answers than wrong ones, then you will get a chance to buy your favorite waterslide, but if you have more wrong answers than right ones, you will have to walk upside down." Spooky wanted a waterslide so badly that he immediately agreed to it. Ever since, he has been walking upside down. He could not answer many questions.

Do not worry, kids; his dad told Spooky that he can build a team, make any kid the captain of his team, and the team can help him clear the mission. If the mission is cleared, Spooky's dad will buy a waterslide for Spooky, and Spooky will be able to walk normally again. Spooky thinks you are very good at math, and you can help him clear the mission. So, Spooky wants you to be the captain.

Are you ready to be the captain of Spooky's team and help Spooky?

I hope you are excited and said "Yes!" Read the next few pages carefully, and then try to complete the mission to help Spooky.

Discovering the Magic of Numbers

Numbers are made of digits. You can use a place value chart to see the place of each digit in a number. Let's look at the chart for number 5,432. As you can see, starting from right to left, 2 is in the ones place, 3 is in the tens place, 4 is in the hundreds place, and 5 is in the thousands place.

5	4	3	2
Thousands	Hundreds	Tens	Ones

Three forms of writing numbers:

1) Standard form is the usual way of writing numbers. Example: 5432.

2) Expanded form is breaking down the numbers in such a way that you see the value of each number. Therefore, the expanded form of 5432 is 5000 + 400 + 30 + 2.

3) Word form is when you write a number the way that you read it. When you see the number 5432, you write it as "five thousand four hundred thirty-two".

Comparing Numbers

You can use a place value chart to compare two numbers. For example, let's say we need to find which number is larger: 465 or 489.

4	6	5
Hundreds	Tens	Ones

4	8	9
Hundreds	Tens	Ones

To compare numbers, compare each digit from left to right, starting with the greatest place value. Since the digits in the hundreds place are the same, let's move to the tens place. Since 8 is larger than 6, it means the number 489 is greater than the number 465, or in other words, 465 is less than 489.

489 > 465 or 465 < 489. See my tip on page 33 if you get confused between the greater than and less than symbols.

Steps for Comparing Numbers

Step 1: Always start from the digits at the highest place value.

Step 2: Compare the digits at this place in both numbers. The number with the larger digit is greater.

Step 3: If the digits are equal, move one place value to the right, and repeat Step 2.

Rounding Numbers

Rounding helps us simplify large numbers, making them easier to work with. In this section we are going to learn how to round numbers to the nearest 10, nearest 100 and nearest 1000.

1) Rounding to the Nearest Ten:

- To round the number to nearest ten, look at the digit in the ones place.

- If it is 5 or greater, round up, if it is less than 5, round down.

Examples:

a) Let's round the number 47 to the nearest ten. Since the digit 7 in the one's place is 5 or greater; therefore, the number 47 will round up to number 50.

4	7
Tens	Ones

b) Now let's round the number 44 to the nearest ten. The digit 4 in the one's place is less than 5; therefore, the number 44 will round down to number 40.

2) Rounding to the Nearest Hundred:

- We round to the nearest hundreds place by examining the tens place.

- If the tens value is between 0 and 4(including 4), the number must be rounded down, and if the tens value is 5 or greater, the number must be rounded up.

Examples:

a) Let's round the number 876 to the nearest hundred. The digit 7 in the ten's place is 5 or greater; therefore, the number 876 will round up to number 900.

8	7	6
Hundred	Tens	Ones

b) Now let's round the number 528 to the nearest hundred. The digit 2 in the ten's place is less than 5; therefore, the number 528 will round down to number 500.

3) Rounding to the Nearest Thousand:

- We round to the nearest thousands place by examining the digit in the hundreds place.

- If this digit value is between 0 and 4 (including 4), the number must be rounded down, and if digit value is 5 or greater, the number must be rounded up.

Examples:

a) Let's round the number 5975 to the nearest thousand. The digit 9 in the hundred's place is 5 or greater; therefore, the number 5975 will round up to number 6000.

5	9	7	5
Thousand	Hundred	Tens	Ones

b) Now let's round the number 6666 to the nearest thousand. The digit 6 in the hundred's place is 5 or greater; therefore, the number 6666 will round up to number 7000.

Exercise:

Round each number to the nearest hundred.

1) 528

2) 666

3) 789

4) 1374

Round each number to the nearest thousand.

5) 24813

6) 5095

7) 7399

Answers: 1) 500 2) 700 3) 800 4) 1400 5) 25,000 6) 5000 7) 7000

Adding 2-Digit Numbers

Shopping with Spooky: A Trip to the Toy Store

Spooky won the annual Scripps Spelling Bee at the school. He had worked very hard for it. Spooky's dad wanted to reward Spooky for his effort. He took Spooky to his favorite toy store. Spooky wanted to buy a big Sonic plush.

He asked his dad, "How much money do you have, Dad?" Dad replied, "Right now, I have 45 dollars in my bag and 33 dollars in my wallet."

As Spooky started looking for a plush, Dad asked, "How much money do you think I have?"

Spooky replied, "Daddy, that's easy to find out. I just need to add 45 and 33. Let me show you how to do it.

First, we add the ones. So, 5 + 3 = 8. Then we add the digits in the tens place. 4 + 3 = 7. So, you have 78 dollars."

	Tens	Ones
Carryover		
	4	5
+	3	3
		8

	Tens	Ones
Carryover		
	4	5
+	3	3
Answer:	7	8

Dad said, "Great job, Spooky. I am so proud of you. This plush is $35, so I am going to buy it for you."

Carryovers

When we add two or more numbers, we first add the digits in the ones place. If the sum of the digits in the ones place is greater than 9, for example 8 + 5 = 13, which is equal to 10 + 3 (**one ten and three ones**). This **one ten** is carried over to the tens place. In this case, 1 is called the carryover. To understand it better, let's look at an example:

We are going to add two numbers: 45 and 38.

In number 45, 5 is in the ones place and 4 is in the tens place. In number 38, 8 is in the ones place and 3 is in the tens place.

	Tens	Ones
Carryover	1	
	4	5
+	3	8
		3

	Tens	Ones
Carryover	1	
	4	5
+	3	8
Answer:	8	3

Step 1) Add the digits in the ones place, so we have 8 + 5 = 13.

Step 2) Since the number 13 is greater than 9, the digit in the tens place will carryover. Therefore, 1 will be our carry over.

Step 3) Finally, add the digits in the tens place and the carryover, so we do 4 + 3 + 1 = 8.

Therefore, 45 + 38 = 83.

Spooky's Addition Adventure at the Bank with His Mom

The next morning, Spooky went to the bank with Mom. The banker asked his mom how much money she wanted to take out. Mom replied, "I need 47 dollars to buy a dress and 35 dollars to pay for the gas." The banker saw Spooky trying to figure out how much money was needed. So, he asked Spooky, "Can you please help us, and tell me how much money I should give to your mom?"

Spooky said, "That's easy to find out. I need to add 47 and 35. Let me show you how to do it."

First, we add the ones. So, 7 + 5 = 12. In the number 12, 2 is in the ones place and 1 is in the tens place. Since 12 is greater than 9, the digit in the tens place will be a carryover. Therefore, 1 will be our carryover.

Next, we add the tens. 4 + 3 + 1(carryover) = 8. So, you need to give us 82 dollars.

	Tens	Ones
Carryover	1	
	4	7
+	3	5
		2

	Tens	Ones
Carryover	1	
	4	7
+	3	5
Answer:	**8**	**2**

Impressed by Spooky's math, the banker gave a lollipop   to Spooky.

Key Points to Remember:

a)   We add the digits in the ones place first.

b)   If the result of adding digits in the ones place is greater than 9, we carry over the digit in the tens place of the result.

c)   Then we add digits in the tens place and add the carryover.

Practice Questions

Practice Questions

TIP: For all practice questions, use a Post-it to cover and attempt the problem.

Let's do some more practice before we try to complete the mission:

a)   Ryan goes for apple picking every year with his family. He has 16 apples in his basket. He picked up 7 more from the ground. How many apples does Ryan have now?

Answer:

	Tens	Ones
Carryover	1	
	1	6
+		7
		3

	Tens	Ones
Carryover	1	
	1	6
+		7
Answer:	2	3

b) A farmer has a basket with 15 oranges, and he goes to the market to buy some more. He buys 17 oranges at the market. How many oranges does the farmer have in his basket now?

Answer:

	Tens	Ones
Carryover	1	
	1	5
+	1	7
		2

	Tens	Ones
Carryover	1	
	1	5
+	1	7
Answer:	3	2

c) Jackson loves collecting Pokémon cards. He already has 25 Pokémon cards in his Pokémon binder. He buys 24 more Pokémon cards from the shop. How many Pokémon cards does he have now?

Answer:

	Tens	Ones
Carryover		
	2	5
+	2	4
		9

	Tens	Ones
Carryover		
	2	5
+	2	4
Answer:	4	9

d) Sophia has 18 stickers and she gets 42 more from her teacher. How many stickers does Sophia have now?

Answer:

	Tens	Ones
Carryover	1	
	1	8
+	4	2
		0

	Tens	Ones
Carryover	1	
	1	8
+	4	2
Answer:	6	0

e) Mike is in 3rd grade. During spring break, his family decided to go from Austin to San Antonio. Mike asked his dad how many miles the drive from Austin to San Antonio is.

Dad said, "From Austin to San Marcos, it is about 37 miles and then from San Marcos to San Antonio is about 39 miles." Then he asked his son "Can you do the math and tell me how many miles it is from Austin to San Antonio?"

Austin ----------37 miles----------→ San Marcos ---------39----→San Antonio

Answer:

To determine the total distance, Mike needs to add the distance from Austin to San Marcos to the distance from San Marcos to San Antonio.'

	Tens	Ones
Carryover	1	
	3	7
+	3	9
		6

	Tens	Ones
Carryover	1	
	3	7
+	3	9
Answer:	7	6

Therefore, it is 76 miles from Austin to San Antonio.

Mission 1

Ready for Mission

It's time to help Spooky. You need to answer at least 10 questions correctly to complete the mission. Answers are provided at the end of the chapter.

1.

	Tens	Ones
Carryover		
	4	7
+	3	2
Answer:		

2.

	Tens	Ones
Carryover		
	2	6
+	5	5
Answer:		

3.

	Tens	Ones
Carryover		
	2	2
+	5	9
Answer:		

4.

	Tens	Ones
Carryover		
	4	0
+	5	1
Answer:		

5.

	Tens	Ones
Carryover		
	8	1
+	0	9
Answer:		

6.

	Tens	Ones
Carryover		
	1	0
+	7	7
Answer:		

7.

	Tens	Ones
Carryover		
	3	5
+	3	5
Answer:		

8.

	Tens	Ones
Carryover		
	1	8
+	1	9
Answer:		

9.

	Tens	Ones
Carryover		
	6	1
+	2	9
Answer:		

10.

	Tens	Ones
Carryover		
	4	9
+	4	9
Answer:		

11. Circle the largest number in the following numbers:

   a. 43

   b. 47

   c. 48

   d. 39

12. Which of the following sequence of numbers is in ascending order (least to greatest)?

   a. 24, 26, 34, 33

   b. 44, 33, 45, 65

   c. 20, 21, 23, 43

   d. 34, 31, 36, 45

13. Megan has 33 pennies, 13 dimes and 16 nickels. How many coins does she have in all?

SHOW YOUR WORK

Answer: Megan has _____ coins.

14. There are 36 adults and 18 kids in the movie theater. How many people are at the movie theater?

SHOW YOUR WORK

Answer: There are _____ people at the movie theater.

15.   Will has 45 marbles. His sister has 39 marbles. How many marbles do they have in all?

SHOW YOUR WORK

Answer: They have _____marbles.

Time to grade yourself. To complete this mission, you need to answer at least 10 questions correctly. You can verify your answers which are provided at the end of the chapter, or you can ask someone in your family to check your work. In the top section of the circle on the next page, write how many you got correct.

Mission 1:

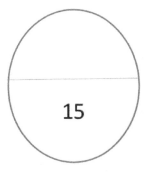

15

If you answered 10 or more correctly, then congratulations! You have earned the following badge. Because of your efforts, Spooky can walk upright and he can get his dream waterslide.

But if you answered fewer than 10 correctly, don't worry! You can try again and still earn the badge while helping Spooky.

Adding 3-Digit Numbers

This section welcomes you to the exciting world of adding 3-digit numbers! In this section, we'll learn the strategies, tips, and tricks to confidently add three-digit numbers together. Get ready for an exciting adventure.

Meet Spooky's Friends

From the left to right:

Megan: Spooky's sweet little sister who is loving, caring and a little bit annoying.

    Her favorite line: "I am better than my big brother."

Arjun: Also known as Little Scientist, always doing dangerous experiments.

    His favorite line: "Mix everything and see what happens."

Odunayo: Known as Mr. Cool. Stress free, and he loves electronics.

    His favorite line: "Keep your cool and you can solve any problem."

Jose: Known as little MJ, loves dancing and singing.

    His favorite line: "Let's dance and party."

Olivia: Spooky's classmate and his best friend.

    Her favorite line: "Be kind to everyone."

Magical Wand

Help Spooky get a magical wand from the best magician in the world. With this wand, Spooky can make it rain ice cream.

Just like most of us, Spooky loves ice cream. Whenever he goes to an ice cream store with his parents, he gets confused. He wants to eat vanilla, chocolate, mint, strawberry, and every flavor they have. He always wishes that he could eat them all.

One day, while Spooky was on his way to school, he saw a person sitting on the corner of the street, looking very sad. Spooky asked him, "Why are you so sad?" The person replied, "I am very hungry. I have not eaten anything in the last two days." Spooky felt bad and decided to help the needy person. He immediately took his lunchbox out and gave it to the needy person. The person said, "I have been standing here for last two days. You are the first person who has helped me. You are so kind. I have a surprise for you. I am not a needy person; I am Luca, the best magician in this world. Make your wish." Spooky got excited and said, "Can you please give me a wand so it can rain ice cream whenever I want?" The magician paused and said, "That's a strange wish. I can do that for you, but I have one condition. For me to grant your wish, you will have to complete a math mission. You need to get at least 10 answers correct in mission 2. You may build a team that can help you in completing the mission. You can make any of your friends, the captain of your team." Spooky thinks you are good at math and wants you to be the captain of his team.

Are you ready to help Spooky?

I hope you are pumped up and said, "Yes!" Before we attempt to complete the mission, let's look at some examples.

Math at the Electronics Shop: Odunayo's Adventure

Like Odunayo, his dad loves electronics. Whenever a new gadget comes into the market, he wants to buy it immediately. He always takes Odunayo with him to the electronics shop. This time, they went to an electronics shop to buy a new phone. Odunayo's dad asked the guy in the shop, "Can you please tell me the cost of this new mobile phone?" The shop guy said, "If you buy just a mobile phone, it is $699. However, we have a very good deal for you if you need more than one phone. If you buy two mobile phones together, the second phone will only cost you an additional $199. And if you also buy a charging wire with them, it will only add $10 to it." Odunayo asked his dad "How much money do we need if we want to buy all three items today?"

Odunayo's Dad said, "That's easy to find out. Let me explain how to do it".

		Hundreds	Tens	Ones
	Carryover	2	1	
Cost of first phone		6	9	9
Cost of second phone		1	9	9
Cost of charging wire	+		1	0
Answer:		**9**	**0**	**8**

Write all three numbers that we need to add in the table, as shown in the picture above. First, we add the ones place digits: 9+ 9 + 0 = 18. In the number 18, 8 is in the ones place, and 1 is in the tens place. Since 18 is greater than 9, the digit at the tens place will be a carryover. So, 1 will be our carryover.

Then we add the tens. 9 + 9 + 1+ 1(carryover) = 20. Again, 20 is greater than 9. So now 2 is the carryover. Finally, we add the digits in the hundreds. 6 + 1 + 2(carryover) = 9.

So, it will cost dad $908 to buy two phones and one charging wire with them.

Key Points to Remember:

a) When adding two or more numbers, start by adding the digits in the ones place.

b) If the sum of adding the digits in the ones place is greater than 9, we get a carryover.

c) Then we add the digits in the tens place and add the carryover from the previous step.

d) Again, if the result of adding digits in the tens place is greater than 9, we get a carryover.

e) Then we add digits in the hundreds place and add the carryover from step d.

Planning Megan's Birthday Party: Addition Adventure

Megan's birthday is coming up in a week. Her parents have decided to throw a big party and invite everyone from Megan's class as well as few of Spooky's friends.

Megan wants everyone to have a lot of fun on her birthday. She told her dad, "Let's get a magician to perform tricks, an ice cream truck for everyone to enjoy their favorite ice cream, and a waterslide. The magician will charge $450, the ice cream truck will cost $230, and the waterslide will cost $135. Can you figure out how much the total cost will be for getting a magician, an ice cream truck, and a waterslide?

Answer: Megan can calculate the total cost of getting a magician, an ice cream truck, and a water slide by adding up the individual costs of each item.

Step 1: Let's add the digits in the ones place.

	Hundreds	Tens	Ones
Carryover			
	4	5	0
	2	3	0
+	1	3	5
			5

Step 2: Is there a carryover when we add the digits in the ones place? Answer is: No.

Step 3: Now, let's add the digits in the tens place.

	Hundreds	Tens	Ones
Carryover	1		
	4	5	0
	2	3	0
+	1	3	5
		1	5

Step 4: Is there a carryover when we add the digits in the tens place? 5 + 3 + 3 = 11. Since 11 is greater than 9, it means there will be a carryover. The 1 in the tens place of 11 will be our carryover.

Step 5: Let's add the digits in the hundreds place and the carryover from step 4.

	Hundreds	Tens	Ones
Carryover	1		
	4	5	0
	2	3	0
+	1	3	5
Answer:	**8**	**1**	**5**

So, it will cost Megan and her family $815 to get a magician, waterslide and an ice cream truck.

Solving the Mystery: A Problem-Solving Adventure

Are you ready to be a detective today? Mrs. Mahany, a 3rd grade class teacher, likes to teach kids how to solve math mysteries. One day, she told her students that if they solve this mystery, then they can get 20 minutes of extra recess. The kids got super excited and started chanting "Let's go, let's go!" So, Mrs. Mahany started the story. She said, "There were three friends, Ryan, Bryan, and Jasper. They had a code language so no one could understand them."

She showed the kids how they used to say digits in their code language:

Number	Code Language
0	n
1	f
2	t
3	o
4	y
5	d
6	g
7	r
8	z
9	u

Then, Mrs. Mahany said, "To give you guys an example, if Ryan says he has "zoo" amount of money, then it means he has 833 dollars." This is because "z" means the digit 8 in their code language, and "o" means 3.

One day, the three friends decided to pool their money together and buy a trampoline.

So, they asked Ryan, "How much money do you have?"

Ryan's answer was "dog."

Then, they asked Bryan, "How much money do you have?"

Bryan said "fun."

Then, they asked Jasper, "How much money do you have?"

Jasper said "toy."

Can you find out if the three friends can buy a trampoline by pooling their money together if the trampoline costs $900 including tax?

Answer: The first step to solve this mystery is decoding the money each friend has. Look at the table above and write down the money each friend has.

3RD GRADE MATH ADVENTURES

Name:	Before Decoding	After decoding
Ryan	Dog	$536
Bryan	Fun	$190
Jasper	Toy	$234

Now we need to find out how much total money they have.

Step 1: First, let's add the digits in the ones place.

	Hundreds	Tens	Ones
Carryover		1	
	5	3	6
	1	9	0
+	2	3	4
			0

Step 2: Is there a carryover when we add digits in the ones place? 6 + 0 + 4 = 10. Since the number 10 is greater than 9, there will be a carryover. Therefore, the answer is: Yes.

You may ask yourself what the carryover will be? So, the sum of the digits in the ones is 10. In the number 10, 1 is in the tens place and 0 is in the ones place. Always remember the digit in the tens place will be the carryover.

Step 3: Now, let's add the digits in the tens place and the carryover from step 2.

	Hundreds	Tens	Ones
Carryover	1	1	
	5	3	6
	1	9	0
+	2	3	4
		6	0

Step 4: Is there a carryover when we add the digits in the tens place? 3 + 9 + 3 + 1 = 16. Since 16 is greater than 9, there will be a carryover. Since 1 is at tens place, 1 will be our carryover.

Step 5: Let's add the digits in the hundreds place and the carryover from step 4.

	Hundreds	Tens	Ones
Carryover	1	1	
	5	3	6
	1	9	0
+	2	3	4
Answer:	**9**	**6**	**0**

So, they have $960 in total. Since the three friends have more money than the cost of the trampoline, they can afford to buy it.

Practice Questions

TIP: For all practice questions, use a Post-it to cover and attempt the problem.

Let's do some more practice before we try to complete our second mission.

1. What is 454 + 132?

	Hundreds	Tens	Ones
Carryover			
	4	5	4
+	1	3	2
Answer:	5	8	6

2. What is 655 + 135?

	Hundreds	Tens	Ones
Carryover		1	
	6	5	5
+	1	3	5
Answer:	7	9	0

3. What is 123 + 155?

	Hundreds	Tens	Ones
Carryover			
	1	2	3
+	1	5	5
Answer:	2	7	8

4. What is 355 + 405?

	Hundreds	Tens	Ones
Carryover		1	
	3	5	5
+	4	0	5
Answer:	7	6	0

5. What is 878 + 23?

	Hundreds	Tens	Ones
Carryover	1	1	
	8	7	8
+		2	3
Answer:	9	0	1

6. What is 666 + 240?

	Hundreds	Tens	Ones
Carryover	1		
	6	6	6
+	2	4	0
Answer:	9	0	6

7. What is 238 + 199?

	Hundreds	Tens	Ones
Carryover	1	1	
	2	3	8
+	1	9	9
Answer:	4	3	7

8. What is 530 + 270?

	Hundreds	Tens	Ones
Carryover	1		
	5	3	0
+	2	7	0
Answer:	8	0	0

9. Horseshoe Falls, which is part of Niagara Falls, is 173 feet high. Akaka Falls, in Hawaii, is 269 feet higher than Horseshoe Falls. What is the height of Akaka Falls?

	Hundreds	Tens	Ones
Carryover	1	1	
	2	6	9
+	1	7	3
Answer:	4	4	2

Adding 4-Digit Numbers

In this section, we will learn how to add 4-digit numbers. Before we begin adding them, let's review the concept of place value. In a 4-digit number, each digit represents a different place value—thousands, hundreds, tens, and ones. Let's take the number 6,427 as an example:

6	4	2	7
Thousands	Hundreds	Tens	Ones

Adding a 4-digits number works the same way as 3-digit number. Let's look at an example. We will add the number 5,535 to 2,575.

We start by adding the ones place: 5 + 5 = 10. Since the sum is greater than 9, we write down the ones place digit (0) and carry over the tens place digit (1).

Then, we add the tens place: 3 + 1 (carried over) + 7 = 11. Again, we write down the tens place digit (1) and carry over the hundreds place digit (1).

Then, we add the hundreds place: 5 + 1 (carried over) + 5 = 11. We write down the hundreds place digit (1) and carry over the thousands place digit (1). In the end, we add the thousands place: 5 + 1 (carried over) + 2 = 8. Therefore, the sum of 5,535 and 2,575 is 8,110.

	Thousands	Hundreds	Tens	Ones
Carryover	1	1	1	
	5	5	3	5
+	2	5	7	5
Answer:	**8**	**1**	**1**	**0**

Let's do some more practice:

1. What is 1234 + 4321?

	Thousands	Hundreds	Tens	Ones
Carryover				
	1	2	3	4
+	4	3	2	1
Answer:	**5**	**5**	**5**	**5**

2. What is 7865 + 1212?

	Thousands	Hundreds	Tens	Ones
Carryover	1			
	7	8	6	5
+	1	2	1	2
Answer:	**9**	**0**	**7**	**7**

3. What is 5032 + 1764?

	Thousands	Hundreds	Tens	Ones
Carryover				
	5	0	3	2
+	1	7	6	4
Answer:	**6**	**7**	**9**	**6**

4. What is 1344 + 3678?

	Thousands	Hundreds	Tens	Ones
Carryover	1	1	1	
	1	3	4	4
+	3	6	7	8
Answer:	**5**	**0**	**2**	**2**

Picture Problems:

1) The picture below shows number of muffins sold at a bakery shop today.

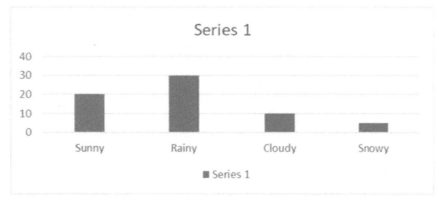

= 10 muffins.

1) How many Blueberry Muffins did the bakery sell? _____ muffins.

2) How many Banana Nut Muffins did the bakery sell? _____ muffins.

3) How many Chocolate chip Muffins did the bakery sell? _____ muffins.

4) How many Lemon Poppy Seed Muffins did the bakery sell? _____ muffins.

5) How many muffins were sold in all? _____ muffins.

Answers: 1) 30 2) 50 3) 20 4) 80 5) 180

2) Bar graph below shows the results of the recorded weather.

Series 1

	Sunny	Rainy	Cloudy	Snowy

■ Series 1

Answer the following questions:

1) How many days were rainy? _____ days.

2) How many more days were sunny than cloudy? _____ days.

3) How many days were Cloudy? _____ days.

Answers: 1) 30 2) 10 3) 10

3) The bar graph shows the number of students in each class.

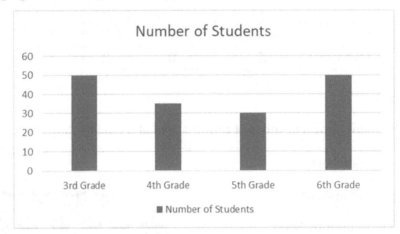

1) How many students are there in the 3rd grade? _____Students

2) How many students are there in the 6th grade? _____Students

3) How many more students are there in the 4th grade when compared to the 5th grade? _____

Answers: 1) 50 2) 50 3) 5

4) The picture below shows the number of seats in different sections in the theatre:

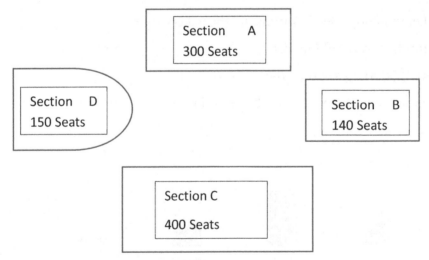

1) How many seats are in sections A and C? _____ seats

2) How many seats are in sections B and D? _____ seats

3) How many seats are in the theatre? _____ seats

Answers: 1) 700 2) 290 3) 990

Mission 2

Ready for Mission

It's time to help Spooky. You need to answer at least 10 questions correctly to complete the mission. If you successfully complete this mission, Spooky will get his magical wand, and you can earn a badge. Good luck!

1.

	Hundreds	Tens	Ones
Carryover			
	3	4	8
+	1	5	1
Answer:			

2.

	Hundreds	Tens	Ones
Carryover			
	1	2	5
+	1	2	5
Answer:			

3.

	Hundreds	Tens	Ones
Carryover			
	5	4	5
+	3	4	5
Answer:			

4.

	Hundreds	Tens	Ones
Carryover			
	0	9	5
+	0	9	9
Answer:			

5.

	Hundreds	Tens	Ones
Carryover			
	7	6	4
+	1	3	5
Answer:			

6.

	Hundreds	Tens	Ones
Carryover			
	1	1	1
+	2	3	8
Answer:			

7.

	Hundreds	Tens	Ones
Carryover			
	7	8	8
+	1	2	2
Answer:			

8.

	Hundreds	Tens	Ones
Carryover			
	1	7	8
+	3	4	5
Answer:			

9.

	Hundreds	Tens	Ones
Carryover			
	2	1	8
+	6	4	5
Answer:			

10.

	Hundreds	Tens	Ones
Carryover			
	4	1	8
+	2	4	5
Answer:			

11. Circle the largest number in the following numbers:

   a) 430

   b) 479

   c) 481

   d) 399

12. Which of the following sequence of numbers is in ascending order (least to greatest)?

   a) 243, 246, 342, 339

   b) 444, 335, 456, 654

   c) 200, 213, 274, 435

   d) 345, 321, 365, 456

13. Circle the smallest number in the following numbers:

   a) 876

   b) 654

   c) 987

   d) 643

14. Which of the following sequence of numbers is in descending order (greatest to least)?

   a) 543, 234, 321, 111

   b) 543, 321, 234, 111

   c) 321, 543, 234, 111

15. Sonic and Amy decided to see how fast they are. Sonic traveled 108 miles in one minute and Amy traveled 88 miles in one minute. How many miles did they travel combined in one minute?

Answer: To find the total distance they traveled we need to combine the distance Sonic and Amy traveled,

$108 + 88 = $ _____ miles.

SHOW YOUR WORK

Time to grade yourself. To complete this mission, you need to answer at least 10 questions correctly. You can verify your answers, or you can ask someone in your family to check your work. In the top section of the circle below, write how many you got correct.

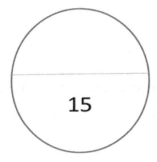

If you answered 10 or more correctly, then congratulations! You have earned yourself the following badge:

Thanks to your efforts, Spooky got the magical wand!

But if you answered fewer than 10 correctly, don't worry! You can try again and still earn the badge and help Spooky.

TIPS

I hope by now you have learned addition and earned two badges. In this section, I will give you some tips so that you can try to solve some addition problems mentally, without using a paper and a pencil.

a) **Tip number 1**: Break down the numbers

Let's say we have to add 64 + 65. We can divide the problem into parts.

We know that 64 = 60 + 4

And 65 = 60 +5.

Therefore, to do 64 + 65, we can add 60 + 4 + 60 + 5

= 60 + 60 + 4 + 5

= 120 + 9 = 129.

Now, try to do 34 + 35 without using paper and a pencil.

b) **Tip number 2:**

If someone asks you a question like this: What is 124 + 125?

And gives you 4 answers to choose from

a)   234

b)   236

c)   244

d)   249

Can you find the answer without using a paper and a pencil? To choose the right answer, you do not need to add the numbers themselves; just add the digits in the ones first. In 124, 4 is in the ones place, and in number 125, 5 is in the ones place. Add the ones. 4 + 5 = 9.

Therefore, we know that when we add 124 + 125, the answer will have a 9 in the ones place. Among the 4 options provided, only option d ends with a 9.

Funny Joke: Why was the math book sad?

Answer: Because it had so many problems.

Answers for Mission 1

1. 79
2. 81
3. 81
4. 91
5. 90
6. 87
7. 70
8. 37
9. 90
10. 98
11. C
12. C
13. 62
14. 54
15. 84

Answers for Mission 2

1. 499
2. 250
3. 890
4. 194
5. 899
6. 349
7. 910
8. 523
9. 863
10. 663
11. C
12. C
13. D
14. B
15. 196 miles

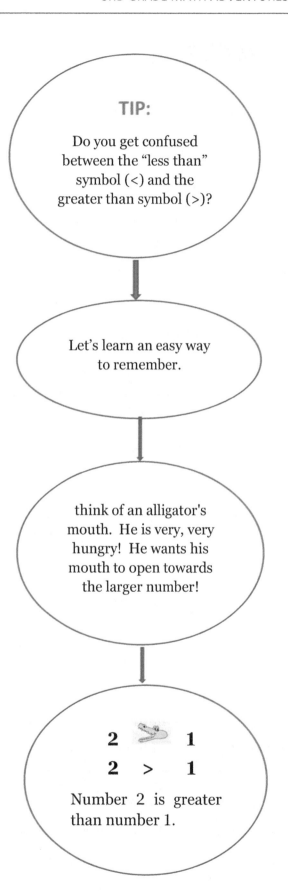

TIP:

Do you get confused between the "less than" symbol (<) and the greater than symbol (>)?

Let's learn an easy way to remember.

think of an alligator's mouth. He is very, very hungry! He wants his mouth to open towards the larger number!

2   1

2 > 1

Number 2 is greater than number 1.

CHAPTER 2

Perimeter

Introduction

Perimeter is the total distance around a shape. For example, let's say there is a rectangular park, and you want to ride your bike around the park once. The total distance that you will ride will be the perimeter. A rectangle has opposite sides equal. So, the total distance you will have to ride your bike is 10 + 4 + 10 + 4 = 28 miles. Therefore, the perimeter of the park is 28 miles.

10 miles

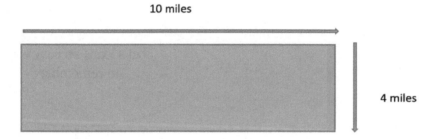

4 miles

Calculating Perimeter

Perimeter of a Triangle

Now look at the triangle below. A triangle has 3 sides. To determine the perimeter of a triangle, we add the length of all the sides. Therefore, the perimeter of triangle will be 4 + 4 + 4 = 12 cm.

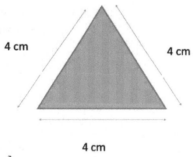

4 cm   4 cm

4 cm

Perimeter of a Quadrilateral

A polygon is a flat two-dimensional shape with straight sides that are fully closed. Triangles and squares are polygons, as well as more complicated shapes like a twelve-sided dodecagon. Polygons are named according to the number of sides and angles they have. We will learn more about them in the "Geometry" chapter.

A quadrilateral is a 4-sided polygon. The perimeter of any quadrilateral is the sum of the lengths of all its sides.

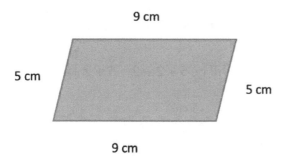

Perimeter of the above quadrilateral = 9 + 5 + 9 + 5 = 28 cm.

a) A trapezoid is a quadrilateral with only one pair of parallel sides. See the picture below.

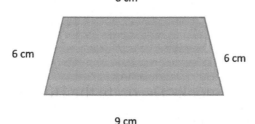

Just like any quadrilateral, the perimeter of a trapezoid is the sum of the length of all its sides. So, for the above trapezoid, the perimeter will be 9 + 6 + 8 + 6 = 29 cm.

b) A rhombus is a quadrilateral with all sides of equal length and opposite sides parallel.

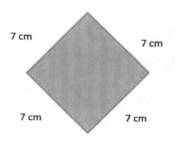

To determine the perimeter of a rhombus, we just need to know the length of one side. For the above rhombus, the perimeter will be 7 + 7 + 7 + 7 = 28 cm.

Perimeter of a Pentagon

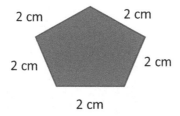

The method of determining the perimeter of any shape remains the same. We add the length of all the sides. A pentagon has 5 sides. So, for a pentagon with all sides 2 cm, the perimeter will be 2 + 2 + 2 + 2 + 2 = 10 cm.

Perimeter of an Irregular Polygon

An irregular polygon does not have all its sides equal. The perimeter of an irregular polygon is also the sum of the lengths of all the sides.

For the polygon shown below, perimeter will be 5 + 2 + 2 + 5 + 2 + 2 + 5 + 2 + 2 + 5 + 2 + 2 = 36 cm

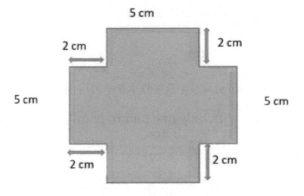

ꞏ Halloween Decorations: Help Spooky Decorate the House

Last year, Spooky's dad decorated the house for Halloween, but Spooky did not like the decorations at all. His dad put blue lights around the windows, which made no sense to Spooky. This year, Spooky wants to decorate the windows himself.

They have 5 windows in the house. All the windows are of same size. Spooky is going to put orange lights around the windows. He went to the store to get lights. The store employee asked Spooky, "What's the perimeter of your window?" Spooky replied, "What's that?" The employee explained that perimeter is the sum of lengths of all sides. So, it is Width of Window + Height of Window+ Width of Window + Height of Window.

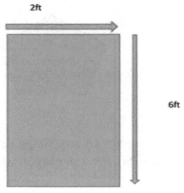

Spooky came back home and measured the width and height of the windows. The width of each window is 2ft and height is 6ft. So, spooky went back to the store and told the same employee, "I measured the windows, and the perimeter of each window is: 2 + 6 + 2 + 6 = 16ft." The store employee gave Spooky five 16ft orange lights.

Mission 3

It's the moment you guys have been waiting for. Impressed by Spooky's house decoration, his dad decided to reward him with a trip to Disney. But before that, Spooky's dad wants to test his ability to calculate perimeter. He said that he would give Spooky some very difficult perimeter questions. Since the questions are so challenging, his dad suggested Spooky could form a team, choose any kid as the team captain, and the team could help him complete the mission. If the mission is accomplished, Spooky can start packing his suitcase for a trip to Disneyland.

Are you ready to be the captain of Spooky's team and help Spooky? You need to answer at least 7 questions correctly to complete the mission. Good luck for this mission! A trip to Disneyland for Spooky and a badge for you is waiting. Let's go get it!

Ready for Mission

Find the perimeter of the following figures.

1.

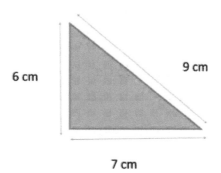

6 cm

9 cm

7 cm

SHOW YOUR WORK

Perimeter = _____cm.

2.

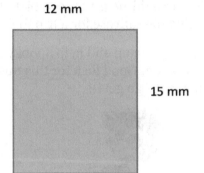

12 mm

15 mm

SHOW YOUR WORK

Perimeter = _____mm.

3.

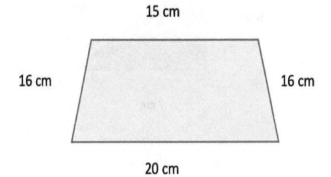

15 cm

16 cm   16 cm

20 cm

SHOW YOUR WORK

Perimeter = _____cm.

4.

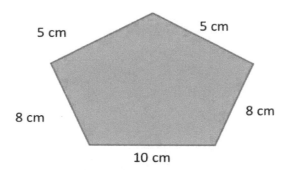

SHOW YOUR WORK

Perimeter =_____cm.

5.

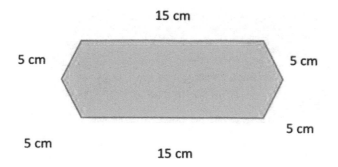

SHOW YOUR WORK

Perimeter = _____cm

6.

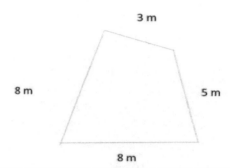

SHOW YOUR WORK

Perimeter =_____m.

7.   Octagon Perimeter

An Octagon has 8 sides.

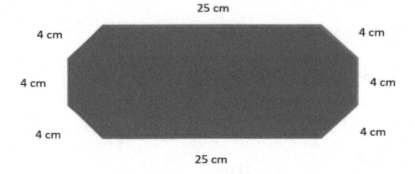

SHOW YOUR WORK

Perimeter =_____cm

8. Perimeter of a trapezoid.

A trapezoid is a quadrilateral with only pair of parallel sides.

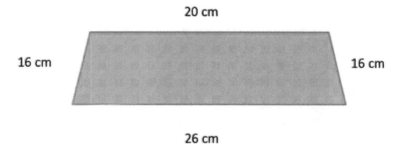

SHOW YOUR WORK

Perimeter = _____cm

9. Perimeter of a parallelogram

A parallelogram is a quadrilateral with two pairs of parallel sides.

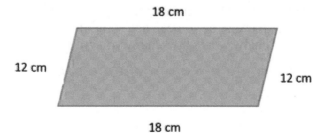

SHOW YOUR WORK

Perimeter = _____cm

10. Perimeter of a square

Note: A square has all sides of equal length.

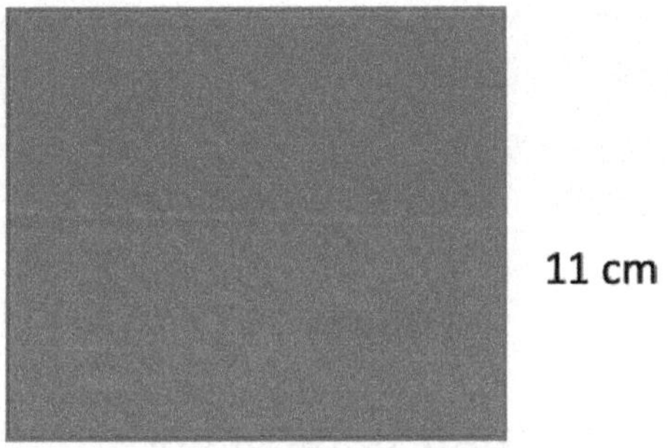

11 cm

SHOW YOUR WORK

Answer: Perimeter of the above square =_____cm

Time to grade yourself. To complete this mission, you need to answer at least 7 questions correctly. You can verify your answers, or you can ask someone in your family to check your work. In the top section of the circle below, write how many you got correct.

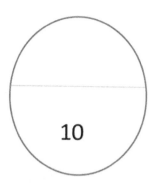

10

If you answered 7 or more correctly, then congratulations! You have earned the following badge:

Thanks to your efforts, Spooky is heading to Disneyland.

But if you answered fewer than 7 correctly, don't worry! You can try again and still earn the badge and help Spooky.

Riddle: You're running a race and at the very end, you pass the person in 2nd place. What place did you finish the race in?

Answer: You finished in second place.

Answers for Mission 3

1. 22 cm
2. 54 mm
3. 67 cm
4. 36 cm
5. 50 cm
6. 24 m
7. 74 cm
8. 78 cm
9. 60 cm
10. 44 cm

CHAPTER 3

Patterns

Introduction

This chapter is one of my favorites. It's all about patterns and having fun with math. We are going to play the role of a detective as we try to identify patterns and solve missing number cases. Let's look at an example:

Find the missing number:

	Column 1	Column 2	Column 3
Row 1	3	7	11
Row 2	2	6	10
Row 3	5	9	??

Goal: Our goal is to find the number that should be in the box with a??

"Let's Get Ready." Wear your detective cap and let's find the missing number.

Look at Row 1. Row 1 has number 3, 7 and 11. How can you reach from 3 to 7? You add 4 to 3.

3 + 4 = 7.

How can you reach from 7 to 11? Again, you add 4. So, it seems that the pattern to get the next number is to add 4 to the current number.

A good detective always confirms first and then only make a conclusion. Let's look at Row 2 and make sure the pattern we have identified works there. The numbers in Row 2 are: 2, 6 and 10.

So, 2 + 4 = 6 and 6 + 4 = 10. Good news! The pattern we identified of adding 4 in Row 1 works in Row 2.

Let's now apply the pattern in Row 3 and find the missing number. 5 + 4 = 9. 9 is already there. Let's add 4 to 9. 9 + 4 = 13. So, the missing number is 13.

3	7	11
2	6	10
5	9	**13**

Great job, Detective!

Are you ready to solve more cases? Now that you know addition so well, I think you can solve these cases.

Case Number 1: Missing Pizza Case

Spooky's friend Arjun ordered 10 Pizzas for his Birthday party, but when he counted them, he found out that one pizza was missing. Someone in the room had already eaten it. There were 20 children in the room. The naughty kid who ate it, left a note that said: if you want to find out who ate the missing pizza, you should find the pattern in the following table and identify the missing number. Once you know the missing number, look around the room. I am wearing a T-shirt with that number on it.

Find the missing number:

11	20	29
8	??	26
14	23	32

Arjun is confused. You are also one of the kids in the party. Arjun needs some help. Can you help? I hope you are now wearing your detective hat and glasses and you are ready to help.

The number is missing in Row 2. So, let's look at Row 1 and Row 3.

Row 1: Numbers are 11, 20, 29. So, how can we reach from 11 to 20? We add 9 to 11. So, 11 + 9 = 20.

Also, 20 + 9 = 29. It looks like the pattern is to add 9 to the previous number.

Row 3: Numbers are 14, 23, 32. Let's confirm our pattern works in row 3. 14 + 9 = 23, 23 + 9 = 32. So, it worked.

Missing Number: So, the missing number is 8 + 9 = 17. Aha, Arjun's friend Bradon is the naughty kid in the room.

Case Number 2: The Tricky Case of a Missing Donut

Spooky's friend Jose is in 3rd grade with Spooky. Miss Clark who is their 3rd grade teacher got 20 donuts for the class. There are 19 kids in the class. So, she got 19 donuts for the kids and one donut for herself. She put the box with donuts on the shelf and went out to get some water. When she came back, she decided to distribute the donuts. After she gave one donut to each kid, she put her hand in the box to get a donut for herself. She was surprised to find out that there were no donuts left. Instead she found a paper in the donut box, that said: "Miss Clark, you are the best teacher and you are my favorite, but I love donuts so much that I could not stop myself. If you want to find me, ask someone in your class to find the missing number. The missing number will give you the clue." Miss Clark laughed. Then she looked at all the kids in the class and chose you and Jose to solve the case.

 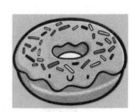  

Note: There may be more than one way to solve this case.

Find the missing number:

22	5	11
40	23	??
58	41	47

So, the missing number is in Row 2 and Column 3. Let's look at Row1 and Row 3.

Row1: The numbers are 22, 5, 11. There seems to be no pattern here. What's happening? Remember the case name is "The **tricky** case of a missing donut". It's tricky, but you have a detective book and page 42 of your book says the following:

"Patterns in a case can be in the rows or in the columns.".

Does that give you any hints? I hope you got some clues. So, the pattern can be in the rows or the columns. We only looked at the rows. Let's look at the columns.

Column 1: 22, 40, 58 – is there any pattern here? Let's find out. How can we reach from 22 to 40? We add 18 to 22. So, 22 + 18 = 40. Now let's add 18 to 40. 18 + 40 = 58. It looks like the pattern is add 18 to the previous number in a column, to get the next number.

Column 2: 5, 23, 41: Let's make sure our pattern holds true for column 2. So, 5 + 18 = 23. 23 + 18 = 41. Yay, looks like we have solved the case.

Missing Number: So, the missing number is 11 + 18 = 29. Who sits at table 29? It is **Chloe**.

Mission 4

It can't get easier than this. You just need to answer one question correctly to complete Mission 4.

Ready for Mission

Case Number 3: Find the Missing Number and Win a Plush

Spooky's friend Odunayo is also in third grade. He went to an amusement park that had a math section where kids could participate in math activities. Odunayo went to the math section with his family. They had a game that offered a prize of a plush toy of your choice if you could find the missing number. Odunayo got excited and asked for the puzzle. It was as follows:

Find the missing number:

110	124	138
76	90	104
62	??	90

Can you help Odunayo win a plush toy? Good luck!

SHOW YOUR WORK

If you answered this question correctly, then congratulations! You have earned the following badge:

Riddle: How many months of the year have 28 days?

Answer: All of them! Every month has *at least* 28 days.

Answer for Mission 4: 76 (Pattern is: Add 14 to get the next number in the row).

CHAPTER 4

Subtraction

Introduction

In the previous chapters, we learned about addition. Addition and subtraction are inverse operations. Subtraction means taking away. For example, if you have 10 candies and you give 4 candies to your friend, then you have 6 candies left.

Subtraction:

10 - 4 = 6

Addition:

6 + 4 = 10

Assisting Spooky: Subtraction Mission for a Basketball Hoop

Spooky has been helping his parents every day and he gets rewarded with stars for all the help. In the last 2 months, he has collected over 240 stars. His parents told him that for every 200 stars, he can buy something. Spooky has been collecting stars with a hope that he can soon buy a new basketball hoop and play with Olivia. However, when he went to a toy shop to buy a present for one of his friend's birthday parties, he got distracted and decided to spend his 200 stars to buy a new board game.

The very next day, Spooky realized that he could no longer buy a new basketball hoop. He became very sad and asked his dad to buy him a new basketball hoop. His dad decided to give Spooky an opportunity to earn extra stars by giving him a mission. He said, "I will give you 2 days to learn about subtraction. After that, I will give you 15 questions and if you can answer 10 of them correctly, then you will earn 160 stars. That will help you to buy a new basketball hoop." Spooky got excited and immediately went to his room to learn about subtraction.

Learning Subtraction with Spooky at the Grocery Store

Spooky and his mom went to grocery store with 80 dollars. They spent 40 dollars on groceries. Now, let's calculate how money they have left.

They had 80 dollars, and they spent 40 dollars. To find out how much money they have left, we need to subtract 40 from 80. So, we need to find out what 80 - 40 is.

First, we subtract the digits in the ones place. 0 - 0 = 0. Then we subtract the digits in the tens place. 8 - 4 = 4. So, they have 40 dollars.

	Tens	Ones
Borrow		
	8	0
-	4	0
		0

	Tens	Ones
Borrow		
	8	0
-	4	0
Answer:	4	0

Borrowing (Regrouping)

When we subtract two numbers, we first subtract the digits in the ones place. Let's consider the example of subtracting 38 from 42. So, we need to find out what 42 - 38 is. Let's start by looking at the digits in the ones place.

	Tens	Ones
Borrow		
	4	2
-	3	8

How can we subtract 8 from 2? Number 8 is greater than number 2.

Number 2 is very sad. However, number 4, who is sitting at the tens place in number 42, decides to help number 2. 4 says, "I am sitting in the tens place. I can give you 1 ten. So, I will become 3 tens, and you will become 12 (10 +2). Will that help?" 2 says: "Yes, that will be a big help." So, now 4 becomes 3, and 2 becomes 12. Now we can subtract 8 from 12.

	Tens	Ones
After Borrow	3	12
	4	2
-	3	8
Answer:		**4**

Then we can subtract the digits in the tens place. Since 4 tens has given 1 ten to the number 2, 4 tens is now 3 tens. Next, we subtract 3 - 3.

	Tens	Ones
Borrow	3	12
	4	2
-	3	8
Answer:	**0**	**4**

Let's look at one more example.

		Tens	Ones
Borrow			
	1	0	0
-		3	8
Answer:			

We have to subtract 38 from 100. Let's start with the digits in the ones place. First, we have to do 0 - 8, but since 8 is greater than 0, we cannot take 8 out of 0. That means, we need to borrow. The 0 in the ones place of number 100, ask its neighbor on the left side, Can I borrow? Since we have another 0 in the tens place, 0 says, I need to borrow first from digit 1 in the hundreds place.

So, 0 in the tens place borrows from 1 in the hundreds place. After the borrowing is done, 1 in the hundreds place becomes 0, 0 in the tens place becomes 10.

		Tens	Ones
Borrow	0	10	
	~~1~~	~~0~~	0
-		3	8
Answer:			

Now, 0 in the ones place can now borrow from the 10 in the tens place. After the borrowing is done, 10 in the tens place becomes 9, and 0 in the ones place becomes 10.

		Tens	Ones
		9	10
Borrow	0	~~10~~	
	~~1~~	0	0
-		3	8
Answer:			

Now, we can do the subtraction.

		Tens	Ones
		9	10
Borrow	0	~~10~~	
	~~1~~	0	0
-		3	8
Answer:		6	2

Waiting for My Favorite Ice Cream: A Math Adventure

Olivia lives in the Belterra community, the fastest growing community in the city of Austin. There are 97 kids between the ages of two and ten. An ice cream truck that comes every Wednesday has a new flavor of ice cream that is driving kids crazy. Not only kids, but some grown-ups are also

having it every Wednesday. The truck usually arrives at 4 p.m. at the rec center. All 97 kids gather there by 3:40 pm to make sure they do not miss the ice cream truck. As they wait for the ice cream truck, they sing this song, "This is my dream, I am waiting for my favorite ice cream." The grown-ups have their own song, but the kids do not like it much. The grown-ups sing, "We are not smelly, please come in our belly."

There are 42 grownups waiting for the ice cream truck. The ice cream truck has 200 cups of the new flavor ice cream. Each kid eats one cup of ice cream and each grownup also gets one cup of ice cream. Can you find out how many ice cream cups of new flavor, the truck is left with?

Let's try to figure out. This will be a 2-step problem.

First let's write down the important points:

a) The truck has a total of 200 ice cream cups of the new flavor.

b) Since each kid eats 1 cup and there are 97 kids in the community, kids will end up eating 97 cups.

c) Grownups will eat 42 cups.

First, we find the total amount of cups that kids and grownups will eat combined = 97 + 42 = 139 cups.

	Hundreds	Tens	Ones
Carryover	1		
	0	9	7
+	0	4	2
	1	3	9

Next, we can find out how many cups the ice cream truck will be left with. We need to take 139 from 200.

	Hundreds	Tens	Ones
Borrow		9	10
Borrow	1	~~10~~	
	~~2~~	0	0
-	1	3	9
Answer:	0	6	1

Uncovering the Pattern: Finding the Missing Number through Subtraction

36	24	12
72	60	??
120	108	96

Goal: Find the number that should be in the box with a ??

Let's get ready by putting on our detective caps and start solving the mystery of the missing stolen number.

Let's look at the numbers in Row 1. They are 36, 24 and 12. Notice that the numbers are decreasing or getting smaller as we move from the right to left. What number should I take from 36 to make it 24? The answer is 12.

Now, what number should I take from 24 to make it 12? Again, it's 12. It seems like the pattern is to get the next number in a row, we subtract 12 from the previous number.

However, a good detective always confirms their findings before making a conclusion. So, let's look at Row 3 and make sure the pattern we have identified works there. The numbers in Row 3 are: 120, 108 and 96.

120 - 12 = 108 and 108 - 12 = 96. Good news! The pattern we identified works in Row 3.

Let's now apply the pattern in Row 2 and find the missing number. 60 - 12 = 48. So, the missing number is 48.

Practice Questions

Practice Questions

TIP: You can cross-check your answer using inverse operation.

Example: **76** - 33 = 43.

To cross-check add 33 to 43.

	3	3
+	4	3
	7	6

Let's do some more practice before we try to complete the mission:

1. Priyanka goes for apple picking every year with her family. She has 76 apples in her basket. Out of the 76 apples, 33 are green apples, and the rest are red apples. How many red apples are there?

Answer:

	Tens	Ones
Borrow		
	7	6
-	3	3
		3

	Tens	Ones
Borrow		
	7	6
-	3	3
Answer:	**4**	**3**

2.   What is 778 - 592?

Answer:

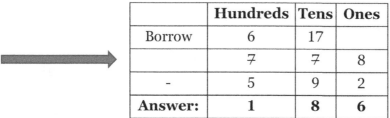

	Hundreds	Tens	Ones
Borrow			
	7	7	8
-	5	9	2
			6

	Hundreds	Tens	Ones
Borrow	6	17	
	7̶	7̶	8
-	5	9	2
		8	6

	Hundreds	Tens	Ones
Borrow	6	17	
	7̶	7̶	8
-	5	9	2
Answer:	1	8	6

3.   What is 4987 - 2346?

Answer:

	Thousands	Hundreds	Tens	Ones
Borrow				
	4	9	8	7
-	2	3	4	6
Answer:	2	6	4	1

4.   What is 4985 - 3476?

Hint: Start with the ones. We cannot subtract 6 from 5. So, the digit 5 must borrow a ten from the digit in the tens place.

	Thousands	Hundreds	Tens	Ones
Borrow			7	15
	4	9	8	5
-	3	4	7	6
Answer:	1	5	0	9

5.   Circular Train: Follow the path and fill the numbers in the boxes. Try it yourself first and then compare your answers with the answer provided below in the second circular train.

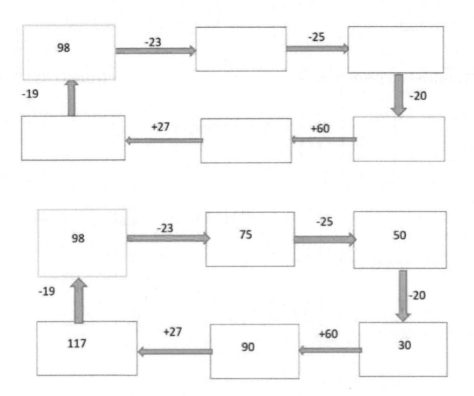

6. Ankit has 946 pennies. Sam has 420 pennies. How many pennies do they have together? Who has more pennies and by how much? Note: This will be a multi-step problem.

Answer: To find out how many pennies they have together, we need to add 946 and 420.

	Thousands	Hundreds	Tens	Ones
Carryover	1			
		9	4	6
+		4	2	0
Answer:	1	3	6	6

Now let's find out who has more pennies. Let's write down both numbers.

Hundreds	Tens	Ones
9	4	6

Hundreds	Tens	Ones
4	2	0

Remember when we compare numbers, we start from the highest place value. So, look at the digits in the hundreds place. Number 946 has 9 in the hundreds place; number 420 has 4. Since 9 is greater than 4, that means number 946 is greater than 420. Therefore, 946 > 420.

The last step is to find out by how much.

	Hundreds	Tens	Ones
Borrow			
	9	4	6
-	4	2	0
Answer:	**5**	**2**	**6**

Ankit has 526 more pennies than Sam.

7. There are 2467 students at the school. 1233 are girls. How many are boys?

Answer: We need to take 1233 out of 2467.

	Thousands	Hundreds	Tens	Ones
Borrow				
	2	4	6	7
-	1	2	3	3
Answer:	**1**	**2**	**3**	**4**

8. Your school is playing another school in your district for the baseball championship. There are 990 seats at the stadium. The stadium is full. There are 500 kids from your school. How many kids are from the other school?

Answer: We need to find out what 990 - 500 is.

	Hundreds	Tens	Ones
Borrow			
	9	9	0
-	5	0	0
Answer:	**4**	**9**	**0**

Mission 5

**Ready for
Mission**

It's time to help Spooky get a new basketball hoop. You need to answer at least 10 questions correctly to complete the mission. If you complete this mission, Spooky will get a new basketball hoop, and you can earn a badge. Good luck!

1.   What is 756 - 325?

	Hundreds	Tens	Ones
Borrow			
	7	5	6
-	3	2	5
Answer:			

2.   What is 458 - 259?

	Hundreds	Tens	Ones
Borrow			
	4	5	8
-	2	5	9
Answer:			

3.   What is 1056 - 786?

	Thousands	Hundreds	Tens	Ones
Borrow				
	1	0	5	6
-		7	8	6
Answer:				

4.   There were 486 red and yellow paper clips in the box. Out of 486, 135 were red. How many were yellow?

SHOW YOUR WORK

        Answer: There were _____ yellow paper clips.

5.   Sophia is one of the best storytellers in the school. She won $300 in the story telling competition. Out of $300, she used $78 to buy a new barbie doll house. How much prize money is she left with?

SHOW YOUR WORK

Answer: Sophia has _____ dollars left.

6. Amy plans to drive 1080 miles to visit her grandparents. She decides she will break the journey into three days. First day she will drive 230 miles, second day she will drive 350 miles. How many miles should she drive third day to reach her destination?

SHOW YOUR WORK

Answer: Amy needs to drive _____ miles to reach her destination.

7. Without using any paper or pencil solve the following:

Given: 1034 + 1048 = 2082.

What is 2082 - 1034?

Answer:

8. Amanda is allowed 400 minutes of electronics time every week. This week, she has already used 245 minutes of it. How many more minutes of electronics is she allowed for the week?

SHOW YOUR WORK

Answer:

9. What is 99 - 25?

	Tens	Ones
Borrow		
	9	9
-	2	5
Answer:		

10. Find the missing number:

30	24	18
60	54	48
48	42	??

SHOW YOUR WORK

Answer:

11. Find the difference between the largest 3-digit number and largest 2-digit number.

    Hint: Largest three-digit number is 999.

    Largest two-digit number is 99.

SHOW YOUR WORK

Answer:

12.   What is 4950 - 2796?

	Thousands	Hundreds	Tens	Ones
Borrow				
	4	9	5	0
-	2	7	9	6
Answer:				

13.   Complete the Grid:

Example: In the grid below, fill the numbers in the 3rd Row and determine the operation we need to do in Operation2 row so we can reach 50. The operation can be either + or -.

	Column 1
Row 1	10
Operation 1	+
Row 2	45
Operation 2	??
Row 3	??
Answer:	50

In the example above, first, we do 10 + 45 = 55. Our goal is to reach 50. That means we need to take 5 away. Therefore, operation 2 will be -, and Row 3 will have 5.

	Column 1
Row 1	10
Operation 1	+
Row 2	45
Operation 2	-
Row 3	**5**
Answer:	50

Now using the above logic, fill the "Operation 2" Row and Row 3.

	Column 1	Column 2	Column 3
Row 1	24	34	24
Operation 1	+	+	-
Row 2	17	18	15
Operation 2	??	??	??
Row 3	??	??	??
Answer:	50	50	50

14. Olivia got a new Magna-Tiles set. There are 150 pieces in the set. She wants to use all the pieces from the set to make a big building. She started making the building. After 20 minutes, her mom asked how many pieces she is left with. She counted and said, I need to use 31 more pieces. Based on the above information, can you find out how many pieces she has used?

SHOW YOUR WORK

Answer:

15. What is 4231 - 1234?

	Thousands	Hundreds	Tens	Ones
Borrow				
	4	2	3	1
-	1	2	3	4
Answer:				

Time to grade yourself. To pass this mission, you need to answer at least 10 questions correctly. You can verify your answers, or you can ask someone in your family to check your work. In the top section of the circle below, write how many you got correct.

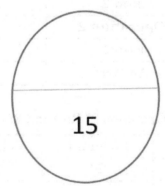

15

If you answered 10 or more correctly, then congratulations! You have earned the following badge:

Thanks to your efforts, Spooky will be getting a new basketball hoop.

But if you answered fewer than 10 correctly, don't worry! You can try again and still earn the badge and help Spooky.

Riddle: What has many keys but can't open any doors?

Answer: A piano.

Answers for Mission 5

1. 431
2. 199
3. 270
4. 351
5. $222
6. 500 miles
7. 1048
8. 155 minutes
9. 74
10. 36
11. 900
12. 2154
13. Operation 2: +,-,+
    Row 3: 9, 2,41
14. 119
15. 2997

CHAPTER 5

Multiplication

Introduction

One day, Spooky came back home from school, feeling very sad and upset. His dad asked him, "What happened?" Spooky replied, "my teacher is launching X-rockets at me." Spooky's dad got concerned and asked, "Rockets"? Spooky explained, "Yes, she keeps asking me what 4 x 3 is." Spooky's dad started smiling and said, "Ah, I understand now. She is teaching multiplication, and you are finding it difficult to understand. Do not worry, son, when I was your age, my parents helped me understand multiplication. I will do the same and help you. Are you ready?" Spooky replied with a hopeful voice, "Yes, Daddy."

Look at the diagram below. I have grouped the balls together. We have 4 groups and each group has 3 balls.

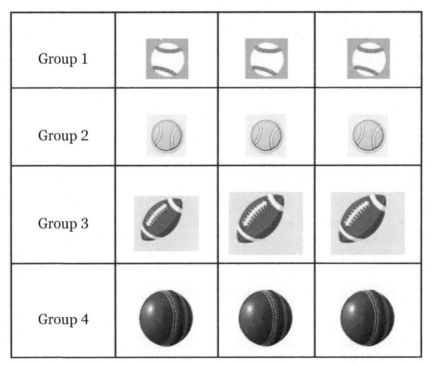

How many total balls are there? Spooky counted them and said 12.

Dad said, "That's right and that's what 4 x 3 is." 4 x 3 means 4 groups of 3.

4 x 3 also means you add three, four times. So, 3 + 3 + 3 + 3 = 12.

Now let's see what 3 x 4 means. It means you add four, three times. So, 4 + 4 + 4 = 12. Therefore, 3 x 4 is same as 4 x 3. This is called **commutative property** of multiplication. According to the commutative property of multiplication, changing the order of the numbers we are multiplying does not change the product.

Example 2

I will give you one more example. Let's say we have to find out what 2 x 7 is? I am going to solve this problem using different methods so that you can understand.

Method 1:

2 x 7 means two groups of seven. So, add the number seven, two times.

Therefore, 2 x 7 = 7 + 7 =14

Method 2:

2 x 7 is same as 7 x 2.

7 x 2 means add the number two, seven times. Therefore, 7 x 2 = 2 + 2 + 2 + 2 + 2 + 2 + 2 =14

Method 3:

We will use lollipops for this example. 2 x 7 means let's create 2 equal groups with each group having 7 lollipops.

Again, if you count them, the total is 14.

Note: The numbers you multiply are called factors. The result is called the product.

2 x 7 = 14

2 and 7 are called factors. 14 is called the product.

Spooky Wants to Start a Lemonade Stand

Spooky wants to make some money before the super bowl game. He wants to give his dad a surprise. His dad who is a big fan of the Kansas City Chiefs, has always wanted to see the Chiefs play in the Super Bowl game. This year the Chiefs are in the Super Bowl. Spooky thought if he makes money, he can give it to his dad, and he can go and watch the game live.

So, Spooky asked his dad, "I want to start a lemonade stand, and I need your help." Dad thought that Spooky wanted to make money to buy a toy for himself. So, he said, "I will only help you if you complete a mission. I will give you some multiplication questions, and if you can answer them correctly, then I will help you open a lemonade stand." His dad told Spooky that the questions are hard, but he can build a team, make any kid the captain of his team and the team can help him clear the mission. Spooky thinks there is no one better than you in multiplication, so he wants you to be the captain of his team.

Are you read to help Spooky?

I hope you jumped in the air and said, "Yes!" Before you help, let's do some practice.

Exploring Multiplication: Multiplying by Various Numbers

In this section we will practice some multiplication questions.

Multiplying by 0

Multiplying any number by a factor of zero is perhaps the easiest of all tasks! No matter what other factor is, when you multiply it by zero, the answer is always zero.

For example: 5 x 0 = 0.

Similarly, 843 x 0 = 0

Multiplying by 1

Multiplying any number by one is perhaps as easy as multiplying by 0! No matter what the number is, when you multiply it by 1, the answer is always the other factor.

For example: 5 x 1 = 5.

Similarly, 800 x 1 = 800.

Multiplying by 10

Multiplying by 10 is also very easy. You just put 0 after the other factor.

For example: **5** x 10 = **50**.

Similarly, **8** x 10 = **8**0.

Multiplying by 2

Multiplying by 2 is not hard at all. You just add the number to itself or double it.

For example: 2 x 5 means add the number five, two times. So, 5 + 5 = 10.

Similarly, 2 x 8 = 8 + 8 = 16.

Multiplying by 9

Multiplying by 9 can be tricky. There are few ways you can handle it.

Let's say we have to do 3 x 9.

Method 1: We know that 3 x 9 means add nine, three times. So, 3 x 9 = 9 + 9 + 9 = **27.**

Method 2: We also know that 3 x 9 = 9 x 3. 9 x 3 means add the number three, nine times. So, 9 x 3 = 3 + 3 + 3 + 3 + 3 + 3 + 3 + 3 + 3 = **27.**

Method 3: There is another way to find out what 3 x 9 is. If you use method 3, you do not even need paper or pencil. We have to multiply 9 with the number 3.

3RD GRADE MATH ADVENTURES

When you have to do multiply by 9, you can first multiply the number by 10 and then subtract the number. This is because 9 = 10 − 1. So, 3 x 9 = 3 x (10 − 1) = (3 x 10) − (3 x 1).

So, to find out what 3 x 9 is

Step 1: Find out what 3 x 10 is. That's easy. We know when multiply by 10, we just put a 0 after the number. So, 3 x 10 = 30.

Step 2: Then subtract the number (Which in this case is 3) from the result of step 1. Therefore, we do 30 − 3, which is **27**.

Note: You can use any of the above methods to find the solution.

Multiplying by 20

It may seem that 20 is a big number and multiplying by 20 may appear difficult. However, let's see how we can make it easy.

First let's look at the number 20. 20 is 2 x 10. Now let's say have to determine what 4 x 20 is.

This is how we can do it:

    a)   20 can be written as 2 x 10

    b)   We first multiply 4 with 2: 4 x 2 =8

    c)   Then we multiply the result from above by 10: 8 x 10 =80

            4 x 20 = 4 x 2 x 10 = 8 x 10 = 80.

Therefore, to multiply a number by 20, we first multiply the number by 2 and then multiply the result by 10.

Multiplying by 30

The same technique can be used when we have to multiply a number by 30.

First, let's look at the number 30. 30 is equal to 3 x 10.

Therefore, to multiply the number by 30, we first multiply number by 3, and then multiply the result by 10.

For example, 2 x 30 = 2 x 3 x 10 = 6 x 10 = 60.

Remember: When you multiply two numbers and if one of the factors or both of them ends with 0's, the easiest way to find the product is, ignore the 0's, multiply the remaining number and then place the appropriate number of 0's at the end of the result.

For example, let's say we need to multiply 200 x 30.

    a)   Number 200 has two zeroes at the end. Without these two zeroes, we are left with the number 2. Let's ignore these two zeroes for now.

    b)   Number 30 has one zero at the end. Without this zero, we are left with the number 3. Let's ignore this one zero.

    c)   So, first multiply 2 x 3. Result is 6.

    d)   Now just put the total number of zeroes we ignored after 6. We ignore two zeroes from number 200 and one zero from number 30. In total we ignored 3 zeroes. Put them after 6.

So, the result is 6000.

That means, 200 x 30 = 6000.

Mastering Multiplication: The Square of a Number

To find the square of any number, we need to multiply the number by itself. For example, to find the square of the number 2, we need to multiply 2 x 2.

Look at the following table to see squares of numbers below 10.

Number	Its square
0	0
1	1
2	4
3	9
4	16
5	25
6	36
7	49
8	64
9	81

Multiplication Makes Movie Night Even More Fun

Spooky and his family decided to go to a movie theater to watch the new released kids' movie. They bought their tickets online. Once they reached the theater, Spooky asked his mom, "How many people could fit in one movie theater?" Mom knew Spooky is learning multiplication. So, she said, "There are 10 rows in each movie theater, and each row has 6 seats. Can you tell me how many people can sit in one movie theatre?"

Spooky said, "Multiplying by 10 is easy. I just need to find what 6 x 10 is."

So, there can be maximum of 6 x 10 = 60 people in the movie theater.

Spooky's Day Out: A Multiplication Adventure

a) Spooky and his 6 friends decided to go to Trampoline Park. They bought the tickets online. Each ticket cost 8 dollars. How much money did they spend on tickets?

Answer: Cost of each ticket is 8 dollars.

Number of friends including Spooky: 7

Number of tickets to buy: 7

Total cost = 8 x 7 = (8 x 5) + (8 x 2) = 40 + 16 = $56.

b) After having fun at Trampoline Park, they all wanted to have ice cream. The cost of each ice cream is 6 dollars. How much money will they end up spending on ice cream? Each kid will eat only one ice cream.

Answer: Cost of each ice cream is 6 dollars.

Number of friends including Spooky: 7

Number of ice creams they will buy: 7

Total cost = 6 x 7 = $42

Practice Questions

Practice Questions

Let's do some more practice before we try to complete our next mission. You can do the multiplication on the paper and compare your answers.

1. What is 3 x 9?

    Answer: Remember: 3 x 9 is same as 9 x 3.

    3 x 9 = 9 + 9 + 9 = 27.

2. What is 4 x 10?

    Answer: When we multiply by 10, we just put one 0 after the other number.

    Therefore, 4 x 10 = 40

3. What is 9 x 9?

    Answer: To determine 9 x 9 either we can add number nine, nine times.

    Or as described previously we can multiply by 10, and then subtract the number.

    So, 9 x 10 = 90.

    9 x 9 = 90 - 9 = 81.

4. What is 5 x 0?

    Answer: Any number multiplied by 0 results in a product of 0.

    Therefore, 5 x 0 = 0

5. There are 7 girls on the stage. Each girl is holding 8 flowers. How many flowers are in all?

   Answer: There are 7 girls on the stage and each girl has 8 flowers. So, total flowers will be

   7 x 8 = 56.

6. There are 5 rows of desks in the class. There are 5 desks in each row. How many total desks are there in the class?

   Answer: Total desks will be 5 x 5 = 25.

7. There are 20 students in each classroom. If there are 4 classrooms, how many total students are there?

   Answer: Total students = 4 x 20 = 80.

8. Ryan made 7 batches of chocolate muffins. There were 5 muffins in each batch. How many total muffins did he make?

   Answer: Total muffin he made = 7 x 5 = 35

9. What is 18 x 10?

   Answer: Always remember, when you multiply by 10, the result is a 0 added to the end of the number.

   So, 18 x 10 = 180.

10. Dylan is training for a 30-mile marathon. She runs 4 miles every day. How many miles will she run in total in 7 days?

    Answer: In 7 days she will run 7 x 4 = 28 miles.

11. What number will make the Equation below true? 46 x ? = 46

    a.) 0

    b.) 1

    c.) 2

    d.) 5

    Answer: b

12. Chloe saves $60 a month for college How much money will she have after 5 months?

    Answer: 60 x 5 = 10 x 6 x 5 = 10 x 30 = $300

13. There are 4 rows of 8 chairs set up for play. How many chairs are set up for play?

    Answer: 4 x 8 = 32 chairs

Properties of Multiplication

If you know 3 x 10 and 3 x 5 then you can easily find out the value of 3 x 15. This is possible because of the distributive property. The distributive property states that when you multiply a factor by two addends, you first multiply the factor with each addend, and then add the sum.

That means if we have to calculate 3 x 15, we can break it up into 3 x (10 + 5) = (3 x 10) + (3 x 5) = 30 + 15 = 45.

Let's look at another example:

We know that 12 = 10 + 2, so

6 x 12 = 6 x (10 + 2)

6 x 12 = (6 x 10) + (6 x 2)

6 x 12 = 60 + 12

6 x 12 = 72.

Now let's look at even harder multiplication. Let's say we need to determine what 8 x 23 is? I know it sounds so difficult, but we must not give up. Let's give it a shot.

8 x 23 = 8 x (20 + 3)

8 x 23 = (8 x 20) + (8 x 3)

8 x 23 = 160 + 24

8 x 23 = 184.

Remember to multiply 8 by 20, we first multiply 8 by 2 and then put a 0 on the end of the product.

Try to do this yourself:

Find what 5 x 11 is.

Hint: 5 x 11 = 5 x (10 + 1)

5 x 11 = (5 x 10) + (5 x 1)

5 x 11 = 50 + 5

5 x 11 = 55.

Mission 6

**Ready for
Mission**

It's time to help Spooky, so he can surprise his dad. You need to complete level 3 to finish this Mission. You will start with level 1. As you clear each level, you move up and go to the next level. As you move up, the questions become harder. If you clear this mission, then Spooky will able to make money by setting up a lemonade stand, and you can earn a badge. Good Luck!

Level 1 Questions

There are 10 questions in Level 1. You need to answer at least 8 questions correctly to reach level 2. **Multiply**

1) $1 \times 1 =?$

2) $0 \times 34 =?$

3) $9 \times 1 =?$

4) $78 \times 0 =?$

5) $2 \times 4 =?$

6) $3 \times 5 =?$

7) $4 \times 4 =?$

8) $8 \times 4 =?$

9) $4 \times 3 =?$

10) $7 \times 3 =?$

SHOW YOUR WORK

After you complete all 10 questions, check your answers. If you answered 8 or more correctly, go to the next level. If you end up getting less than 8 correct, then reread the chapter on multiplication and try level 1 again. Good Luck!

Level 2 Questions

There are 10 questions in Level 2. You need to answer at least 7 questions correctly to reach level 2.

Multiply

1. 2 x 4 =?
2. 12 x 10 =?
3. What is the square of 10?
4. 4 x 9 =?
5. 5 x 7 =?
6. Jackson bought 3 bags of potatoes. There are 6 potatoes in each bag. How many potatoes did Jackson buy?
7. Is this true or false?

    9 x 8 = 8 x 9
8. There are 4 quarters in one dollar. How many quarters will be there in 7 dollars?
9. Is this true or false?

    8 x 8 = 8 + 8 + 8 + 8 + 8 + 8 + 8 + 8
10. 9 x 7 =?

SHOW YOUR WORK

You can write your answers on a piece of paper or in the "Show Your Work" section above. After you complete all 10 questions, check your answers. If you answered 7 or more correctly, go to level 3. But if you answered fewer than 7 correctly, then reread the chapter on multiplication and try level 2 questions again.

Level 3 Questions

There are 10 questions in Level 3. You need to answer at least 7 questions correctly to complete this mission.

1. I am a number. My square is 36. What am I?

2. Using the distributive property find what 5 x 11 is?

3. What is 14 x 10?

4. Is this true or false?

   8 x 19 = 8 x (10 + 9)

5. Is this true or false?

   8 x 14 = (8 x 7) + (8 x 7)

6. What is 9 x 9?

7. What is 8 x 8?

8. What is 8 x 20?

9. What is 9 x 30?

10. What is 20 x 20?

SHOW YOUR WORK

If you answered 7 or more correctly, then congratulations! You have earned the following badge:

Thanks to your efforts, Spooky can start a lemonade stand, make some money, and surprise his dad.

But if you answered fewer than 7 correctly, don't worry! You can try again and still earn the badge while helping Spooky.

Riddle: What is easier to get into than out of?

Answer: Trouble

Answers for Mission 6

Level 1 Answers:

1. 1
2. 0
3. 9
4. 0
5. 8
6. 15
7. 16
8. 32
9. 12
10. 21

Level 2 Answers:

1. 8
2. 120
3. 100
4. 36
5. 35
6. 18
7. True
8. 28
9. True
10. 63

Level 3 Answers:

1. 6
2. 5 x 11 = (5 x 10) + (5 x 1) = 50 +5 = 55
3. 140
4. True
5. True
6. 81
7. 64
8. 160
9. 270
10. 400

CHAPTER 6

Area

Introduction

Area is the amount of space a flat shape or surface takes up. Look at the rectangle below. How much space does this rectangle take up? To find that out let's find the area of this board.

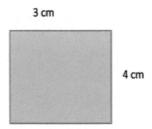

3 cm

4 cm

To find the area of a **grid,** such as rectangle or a square, you **multiply** the **length** by the **width**. So, for the rectangle above, the area is calculated as follows: Area = 3 x 4 = 12 cm². In this case, the length and width are measured in centimeters, so the area will be in square centimeters and is written as cm².

Let's look at some more examples:

Area of a Square

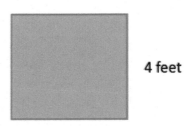

4 feet

A square has equal sides. So, the area of a square will 4 ft x 4 ft = 16 ft².

Area of a L shaped Figure

We know how to find area of a rectangle or a square. Let's see how we can find area of a L shaped figure.

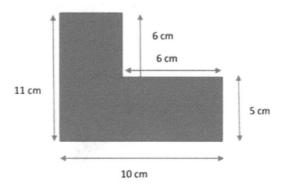

Step 1: Find the missing length.

First, we need to find the missing length.

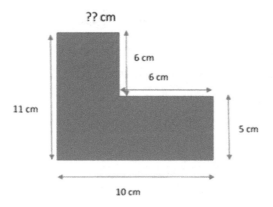

The missing length is 10 cm − 6 cm = 4 cm.

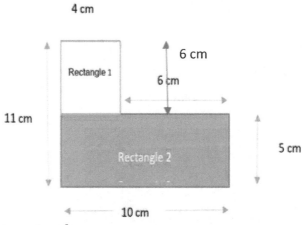

Step 2: Divide L shape into rectangles.

Step 3: Calculate area of rectangle 1 and rectangle 2

Area of Rectangle 1 = 6 x 4 = 24 cm²

Area of Rectangle 2 = 10 x 5 = 50 cm²

Step 4: Add the area of rectangle 1 and rectangle 2 to get area of L shaped figure

Area of L shaped figure = 24 + 50 = 74 cm²

Practice Questions

Practice Questions

1. Find the area of a square with one of its sides being 6 cm.

    Answer: Area of square = 6 cm x 6 cm = 36 cm².

2. Find the area of the following rectangle:

    6 cm

    7 cm

    Answer: Area of the above rectangle = 6 cm x 7 cm = 42 cm².

3. Find the area of the following rectangle:

    9 cm

    7 cm

    Answer: Area of above rectangle = 9 cm x 7 cm = 63 cm².

4. Find the area of the following L shape figure:

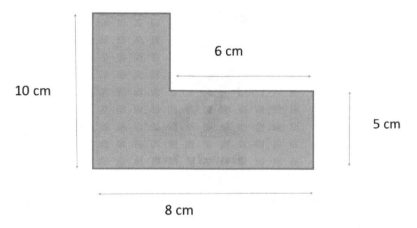

Answer: Divide the L shape into 2 rectangles.

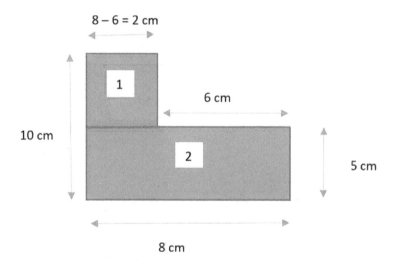

Length of Rectangle 1: = 8 − 6 = 2 cm.

Width of Rectangle 1: = 10 − 5 = 5 cm.

Area of Rectangle 1 = 2 x 5 = 10 cm²

Area of Rectangle 2 = 8 x 5 = 40 cm²

Area of L shaped figure = 10 + 40 = 50 cm²

Mission 7

Ready for Mission

It's time to help Spooky get another present. You need to answer at least 7 questions correctly to pass this mission. If you clear this mission, then Spooky will able to get another present, and you can earn a badge. Good luck!

Answer the following questions:

1. Find the area of a square with a side length of 5 cm.

SHOW YOUR WORK

Answer:

2. Sarah wants to put a rectangular rug in her room. The length of the rug is 5 feet, and the width is 3 feet. What is the area of the rug?

SHOW YOUR WORK

Answer:

3. Find the area of a square with a side length of 10 cm?

SHOW YOUR WORK

Answer:

4.   Find the area of a rectangle with one side 7 cm and other side 6 cm?

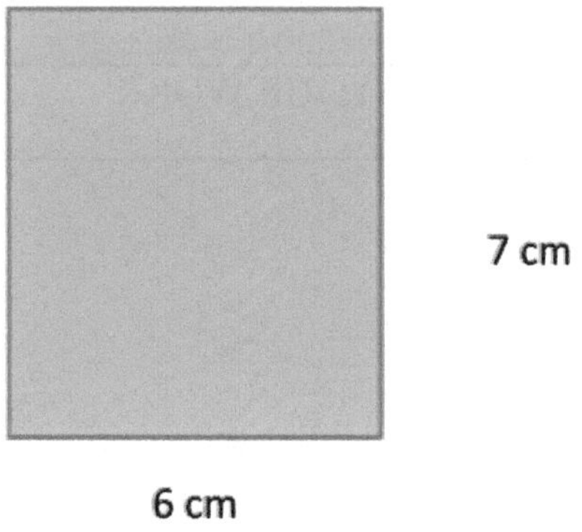

7 cm

6 cm

SHOW YOUR WORK

Answer:

5.   Find the area of the following L Shape:

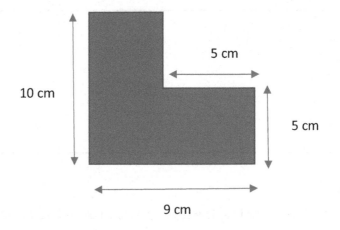

SHOW YOUR WORK

Answer:

6.   Find the area of a square with a side of 4 cm.

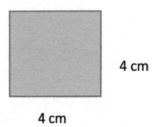

4 cm

4 cm

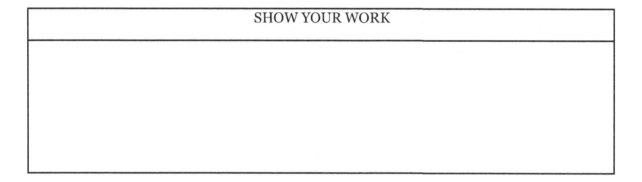

Answer:

7. A garden in a park has a rectangular shape. The length of the garden is 8 meters, and the width is 4 meters. What is the area of the garden?

SHOW YOUR WORK

Answer:

8. Find the area in unit squares.

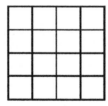

Answer:

9. Find the area of the following L Shape:

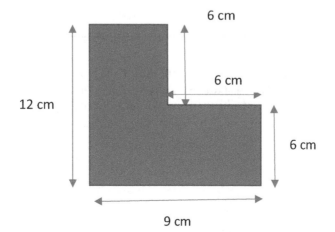

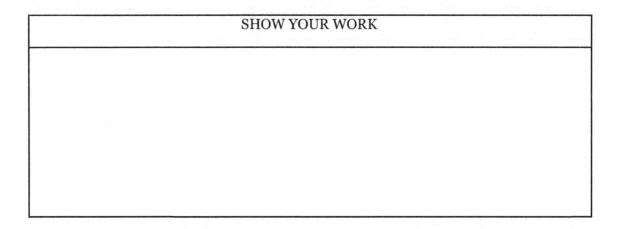

Answer:

10. Find the area of the following Shape:

    Hint: draw lines to divide the shape into rectangles

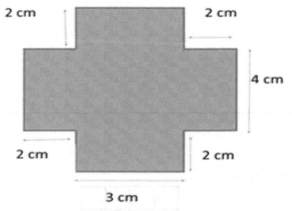

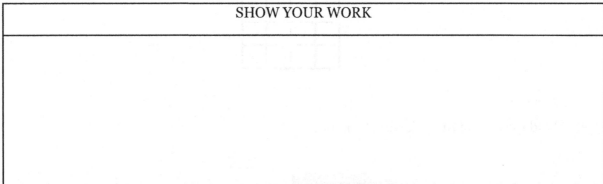

Time to grade yourself. To pass this mission, you need to answer at least 7 questions correctly. You can verify your answers, or you can ask someone in your family to check your work. In the top section of the circle below, write how many you got correct.

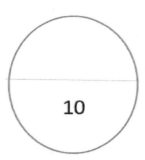

If you answered 7 or more correctly, then congratulations! You have earned the following badge:

Thanks to your efforts, Spooky will get another present.

But if you answered fewer than 7 correctly, don't worry! You can try again and still earn the badge and help Spooky.

Riddle: The more you take, the more you leave behind. What are they?

Answer: Footsteps.

Answers for Mission 7

1. 25 cm²
2. 15 ft²
3. 100 cm²
4. 42 cm²
5. 65 cm²
6. 16 cm²
7. 32 m²
8. 16 un²
9. 72 cm²
10. 40 cm²

CHAPTER 7

Odd, Even Numbers, and More

Learning About Odd and Even Numbers

Odd numbers are those numbers that cannot be divided into two whole equal parts, whereas even numbers are those numbers that can be divided into two equal parts. If a number can be divided by 2 then it's an even number.

Example: Is number 10 even or odd?

Can we reach 10 by multiplying any number with 2?

Yes, we can. 2 x 5 = 10. That means 10 is an even number.

TIP:

An easy way to remember is that if a number has 0, 2, 4, 6, 8 in the ones place, it is an even number. On the other hand, if a number has 1, 3, 5, 7, 9 in the ones place, it is an odd number.

Is 245678 even or odd?

We don't worry about how big the number is. Just look at the digit in the ones place. We see the digit 8. Therefore, it's an even number.

Is 99999989 even or odd?

Again, just look at the digit in the ones place. We see the digit 9. Therefore, it's an odd number.

Fun Facts:

a)   If we add an odd number to an even number, will the sum be odd or even?

  We do not need to remember this. We can easily find out.

  Choose any odd number: Let's say 3.

  Choose any even number: Let's say 4.

  Add them: 3 + 4 = 7.

  Therefore, if we add an odd number to an even number, we get an odd number.

b)   Add an even number to an even number. Will the result be odd or even?

  Choose any even number: Say 6.

  Choose another even number: Say 4. Add them: 6 + 4 = 10.

  So, if we add an even number to an even number, we get an even number.

c)   Add an odd number to an odd number. Will the result be odd or even?

  Choose any odd number: Say 7.

  Choose another odd number: Say 3. Add them: 7 + 3 = 10.

  So, if we add an odd number to an odd number, we get an even number.

d)   Multiply an odd number with another odd number. Will the result be odd or even?

Choose any odd number: Say 7.

Choose another odd number: Say 3. Multiply them: 7 x 3 = 21.

So, if we multiply an odd number with another odd number, the result will be an odd number.

e)   Multiply an odd number with an even number. Will the result be odd or even?

Choose any odd number: Say 7.

Choose any even number: Say 4. Multiply them: 7 x 4 = 28.

So, if we multiply an odd number with an even number, we get an even number.

f)   Multiply an even number with an even number. Will the result be odd or even?

Choose any even number: Say 8.

Choose another even number: Say 4. Multiply them: 8 x 4 = 32.

So, if we multiply an even number with another even number, we get an even number.

Reach Me if You Can: A Multiplication Challenge

Spooky's dad got a present for Spooky and decided to hide it in the house and let Spooky find it. After hiding the present at a place where Spooky has to use a ladder, Spooky's dad put fake signs "Reach me if you can" all around the house. He told Spooky, only one sign has the present behind it. Can you find it?

Spooky started moving the ladder from one place to another. After searching for about 30 minutes, he finally found the sign behind which the present was hidden. Spooky was very excited, but at the same time, he was tired. He opened his present and started playing with it. After some time, Spooky's dad came and said, "Do you wish there were some hints, so you do not have to go to every sign?" Spooky said, "Yes, Dad." Then his dad said, "Do you want to learn something new today? If you want to earn another present, then you will have to complete a mission that I will give you. The mission will have 5 questions, and you need to answer at least 3 correctly. Since you are going to learn something new, and I want to give you a fair chance, I will let you build a team, make any kid the captain of you team, and the team can help you complete the mission. Are you up for the challenge?" What do you think Spooky said? "Of course," he said, "Yes!" After all, who does not want a present?

Can Number 2 Reach Me? Exploring Multiples in Multiplication

We have learned how to determine whether a number is even or odd. The next question is how to check if a number is a multiple of 2. This means that if we are given a number like 10, we ask ourselves, "Can 2 reach 10?" In other words, can we multiply a number by 2 to get to the product 10? We know that 2 multiplied by 5 equals 10, so the answer is yes, 2 can reach 10. In other words, 10 is a multiple of 2.

The easiest way to determine if a number can be reached by 2 is by checking if it is even or odd. If a number is even, it can be reached by 2. However, if a number is odd, it cannot be reached by 2.

Example 1: Is number 74 a multiple of 2?

Answer: First, we need to determine whether 74 is an even or odd number. Let's look at the digit in the ones place of number 74. We know that any number that has 0, 2, 4, 6, 8 in the ones place is an even number. Since 74 has 4 in the ones place, it is an even number. Therefore, it is a multiple of 2.

2 x 37 = 74.

Example 2: Is number 85 a multiple of 2?

Answer: First, we need to determine whether 85 is an even number or odd number. Let's look at the digit in the ones place of number 85. We know any number that has 0,2,4,6,8 in the ones place is an even number. Since 85 has 5 in the ones place, it is an odd number. Therefore, it is not a multiple of 2.

Can number 3 reach me

We learned how we can we find out if a number is a multiple of two or not. Now we will see how to check if a number can be reached by 3. If the sum of the digits of a number is a multiple of 3, then the number can be reached by 3. Let's look at an example:

Example 1: Can number 342 be reached by 3?

To determine if the number 342 can be reached by 3, we first need to add all its digits together. So, we add 3 + 4 + 2 = 9. Now, can 9 be reached by 3? Yes, it can be (3 x 3 = 9).

Therefore, we can say that 342 is a multiple of 3.

Example 2: Can number 987 be reached by 3?

To determine if the number 987 can be reached by 3, first add all the digits of number 987. So, we add 9 + 8 + 7 = 24. Since 24 can be reached by 3, that means 987 can be reached by 3.

Mission 8

Ready for Mission

You need to answer at least 3 questions correctly to pass this mission. Good Luck! Answer the following questions:

1. Is 87,545 an even number or an odd number?

    Answer:

2. If you add two odd numbers, is the result an odd number or an even number?

SHOW YOUR WORK

Answer:

3. Is 345,654 an even number or an odd number?

    Answer:

4. The sum of three numbers is an even number. Out of these 3 numbers, 2 numbers are odd. Is the 3rd number even or odd?

SHOW YOUR WORK

Answer:

5. Is 9080 an even number or an odd number?

    Answer:

Time to grade yourself. To pass this mission, you need to answer at least 3 questions correctly. You can verify your answers, or you can ask someone in your family to check your work. In the top section of the circle below, write how many you got correct.

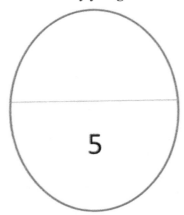

If you answered 3 or more correctly, then congratulations! You have earned the following badge:

Riddle: There's only one word in the dictionary that's spelled wrong. What is it?

Answer: The word "wrong." It's the only word that's spelled W-R-O-N-G.

Answers for Mission 8

1. Odd number
2. Even number
3. Even number
4. Even number
5. Even number

FOR AMBITIOUS STUDENTS:

1) How to determine if a number is divisible by 6. In other words, can 6 reach a number?

Let's take the example of determining whether the number 888 is a multiple of 6.

To see if a number is divisible by 6, we need to check if the number its divisibility by both 3 and 2. The number 888 has 8 in the units place, indicating that it is an even number. Therefore, 2 can reach it.

To determine if 3 can reach it, let's calculate the sum of its digits: 8 + 8 + 8 = 24.

Since, 24 is divisible by 3, therefore 888 can be reached by 3.

Note: 6 x 148 = 888

Now, let's try it yourself: Is the number 788 divisible by 6?

2) How to determine if a number is divisible by 4. In other words, can 4 reach a number?

Let's take the example of determining whether the number 820 is a multiple of 4. A whole number is said to be divisible by 4 if either the last two digits of the number are zeroes or if the last two digits of the number are divisible by 4.

In the number 820, last two digits are 20. Is 20 divisible by 4? Yes, 5 x 4 = 20.

Therefore, the number 820 is divisible by 4. In other words, 4 can reach 820.

3) Let's explore how we can determine if a number can be divided by 9, or in other words, the number is a multiple of 9.

If the sum of the digits of the number is divisible by 9, then the number itself is divisible by 9. Now, let's apply this concept to the number. Is the number 7209 divisible by 9?

The sum of its digits is equal to 7 + 2 + 0 + 9 = 18. Since18 is divisible by 9, we can conclude that 7209 is divisible by 9.

4) Finally, let's see how we can determine if the number is divisible by 5.

If the last digit of a number is 0 or 5, the number is divisible by 5. Consider the number 5544446**5**. While it may be large, our focus is solely on its last digit (at the unit place), which is 5. Therefore, we can conclude that 55444465 is divisible by 5.

CHAPTER 8

Division

Introduction

Division involves splitting a number into equal parts or groups. It is the opposite or inverse of multiplication. We know that 4 x 3 is equal to 12. What if you have 12 apples and you need to divide them into 3 equal groups?

How can we divide these 12 apples into 3 groups?

Step 1: Let's start by putting one apple in each group. We first put one apple in Group 1, then one in group 2 and then one in group 3.

Step 2: Determine how many apples are left. Out of 12 apples, we have placed 3 apples. So, we are left with 9.

Step 3: If we have apples left then repeat step 1

After you are left with no apples, each group will have 4 apples each.

Group1

Group2

Group3

So, when we divide 12 apples into 3 groups, each group gets 4 apples. That's what division is. We can say $12 \div 3 = 4$

Let's look at another example: what is $21 \div 3$?

We can find the solution to this problem using different methods.

Method 1: Make equal groups.

$21 \div 3$ means divide 21 into 3 equal groups. Let's assume we have to divide 21 apples into 3 groups. Let's start by putting one apple in each group. Then we repeat the process. After we put all the apples, we see that each group has 7 apples. So, that means $21 \div 3 = 7$.

Group 1	🍎🍎🍎🍎🍎🍎🍎
Group 2	🍎🍎🍎🍎🍎🍎🍎
Group 3	🍎🍎🍎🍎🍎🍎🍎

Method 2: Division is the inverse of multiplication.

Do we know three times what number is 21?

$3 \times ? = 21$

Let's see

3 x 1 = 3	3 x 2 = 6	3 x 3 = 9	3 x 4 = 12
3 x 5 = 15	3 x 6 = 18	**3 x 7 = 21**	

So, 3×7 is 21. Therefore, $21 \div 3 = 7$.

Note:

In a division sentence, the dividend is the amount that is being divided. The divisor is the number you divide by. The answer is called the quotient.

Spooky's Desire: A Pet Hamster

A 3rd grade teacher bought a hamster for the class. She wanted the kids to have some fun and play with the hamster. When Spooky saw the hamster playing in the hamster wheel, he immediately fell in love with the idea of having a hamster as a pet. He went back home and asked his mom. "Mom, can we please have a hamster as a pet?" His mom replied, "Before I answer that, please tell me how your math test was today?" Spooky said, "I did not do well on my math test. Division is very hard." His mom comforted him and said, "Don't worry, Spooky, we can help you with division. Over the next week, I will teach you division. If you work hard and complete a mission, then we can go to a pet store and get a hamster as a pet. I will give you 15 division questions, and if you can answer 10 or more correctly, then we can go to the pet store." Mom said, "Some questions in the mission will be hard, so you can build a team, make any kid the captain of the team to help complete this mission." Spooky thinks there is no one better than you in division, so he wants you to be the captain of his team.

Are you read to help Spooky?

I hope you jumped in the air and said "Yes!" Before you help, let's do some practice.

Exploring Division: Dividing By Various numbers

In this section we will practice some division questions.

Dividing By 1

Dividing any number by one is perhaps the easiest of all tasks! No matter what the number is, when you divide it by one, the answer is always the number itself.

For example: 12 ÷ 1 = 12

1654 ÷ 1 = 1654

Dividing By 10

Dividing any number that has 0 in the ones place by 10 is easy. To determine the result, just remove 0 from the ones place in the number.

Example 1: 60 ÷ **10** = **6** (Remove 0 from 60).

Note: 6 x 10 = 60.

Example 2: 90 ÷ **10** = 9 (Remove 0 from 90).

Note: 9 x 10 = 90.

Example 3: 300 ÷ **10** = 30(Remove one 0 from 300).

Note: 30 x 10 = 300.

Dividing By 2

Dividing by 2 means splitting the number into two equal groups.

Example: 6 ÷ **2** = **3 (divide 6 into 2 equal parts).**

18 ÷ 2 = 9 (Divide 18 into two equal parts).

Fun Facts:

Let's look at what we can do with the numbers 3, 7, and 21.

3 x 7 = 21

7 x 3 = 21

3 x 7 = add number seven three times = 7 + 7 + 7 = 21

7 x 3 = add number three seven times = 3 + 3 + 3 + 3 + 3 + 3 + 3 = 21

21 ÷ 3 = divide 21 into 3 groups = 7

21 ÷ 7 = divide 21 into 7 groups = 3

Practice Questions

Practice Questions

1.   Write a multiplication sentence and a division sentence for the following models

Model 1:

Answer: There are two rows in the above model. Each row has 4 apples.

2 x 4 = 8

8 ÷ 2 = 4

Model 2:

Answer: There are three rows in the above model. Each row has 3 apples.

3 x 3 = 9

9 ÷ 3 = 3

Model 3:

Answer: There are four rows in the above model. Each row has 6 apples.

$4 \times 6 = 24$

$24 \div 4 = 6$

2. Divide

a) $14 \div 2 = ?$

b) $20 \div 4 = ?$

c) $30 \div 6 = ?$

d) $25 \div 5 = ?$

e) $45 \div 5 = ?$

f) $40 \div 10 = ?$

Answers:

a) 7

b) 5

c) 5

d) 5

e) 9

f) 4

3. A store sells pencils in a pack of 3. Ryan bought 36 pencils in all, how many packs of pencils did he buy?

Answer: Total pencils Ryan Bought: 36

Number of pencils in each pack: 3

Total number of packs he bought = $36 \div 3 = 12$.

4. There are 24 stickers and they are to be divided equally among 8 children. How many stickers will each child get?

Answer: Total stickers: 24

Number of children: 8

Number of stickers each child will get = $24 \div 8 = 3$.

5. If there are 21 marbles and they are to be divided equally among 7 children, how many marbles will each child get?

Answer: Each child will get 3 marbles.

Explanation: To divide the marbles equally among the children, we need to perform division. So, we can write this problem as $21 \div 7 = ?$ When we do this, we get 3. So, each child will get 3 marbles.

6. A chef needed to put 30 plates away in the kitchen. She put the plates in stacks of 10. How many stacks did the chef make?

Answer:

Number of plates = 30

Stack size = 10

Number of plates in each stack = 30 ÷ 10 = 3.

7. There are 48 cupcakes and 6 friends want to share them equally, how many cupcakes will each friend get?

    Answer:

    Number of cupcakes = 48

    Number of friends = 6

    Number of cupcakes each friend will get = 48 ÷ 6 = 8.

8. Samantha has 12 candies and wants to share them equally with her 3 friends. How many candies will each person get?

    Answer:

    Number of candies = 12

    Number of persons including Samantha = 4

    Number of candies each friend will get = 12 ÷ 4 = 3.

9. Tom has 24 pencils that he wants to share equally among 6 friends. How many pencils will each friend get?

    Answer:

    Number of pencils = 24

    Number of friends = 6

    Number of pencils each friend will get = 24 ÷ 6 = 4.

10. Amanda bought 8 dolls. She spent $56 on the dolls. Each doll cost the same amount. What was the cost of each doll?

    Answer: Cost of each doll = 56 ÷ 8 = $7.

11. Arjun has 72 books placed equally on 4 shelves. How many books are on each shelf?

    Answer: Number of books on each shelf = 72 ÷ 4 = 18.

Mission 9

Ready for Mission

It's time to help Spooky get a new pet. You need to answer at least 10 questions correctly to complete this mission. If you clear this mission, then Spooky will able to go to the pet store and get a hamster. Good Luck!

Fun Fact: Hamsters are nocturnal. They are active at night.

Answer the following questions:

1. If you have 21 candies and you want to share them equally among 7 friends, how many candies will each friend get?

SHOW YOUR WORK

Answer:

2. Sam has 36 crayons and he wants to divide them equally into 6 boxes. How many crayons will be in each box?

SHOW YOUR WORK

Answer:

3. There are 24 cookies and 8 people who want to share them equally. How many cookies will each person get?

SHOW YOUR WORK

Answer:

4. If you have 15 pencils and you want to put them in 3 equal groups, how many pencils will be in each group?

SHOW YOUR WORK

Answer:

5. A pizza has 12 slices. If you want to share the pizza equally among 4 people, how many slices will each person get?

SHOW YOUR WORK

Answer:

6. There are 36 flowers and you want to put them into 9 vases equally. How many flowers will be in each vase?

SHOW YOUR WORK

Answer:

7. There are 48 marbles and you want to divide them equally among 6 jars. How many marbles will be in each jar?

SHOW YOUR WORK

Answer:

8. If you have 20 toy cars and you want to divide them equally among 5 children, how many toy cars will each child get?

SHOW YOUR WORK

Answer:

9. There are 45 students and 9 classrooms. If you want to divide the students equally into the class- rooms, how many students will be in each classroom?

SHOW YOUR WORK

Answer:

10. A bag of candy has 36 pieces. If you want to divide the candy equally among 12 kids, how many pieces of candy will each kid get?

```
SHOW YOUR WORK




```

Answer:

11. There are 27 fish in an aquarium. If you want to put them into 3 equal groups, how many fish will be in each group?

```
SHOW YOUR WORK




```

Answer:

12. If there are 35 apples and you want to divide them equally among 5 baskets, how many apples will be in each basket?

```
SHOW YOUR WORK




```

Answer:

13. A pack of gum has 45 pieces. If you want to divide them equally among 5 kids, how many pieces of gum will each kid get?

SHOW YOUR WORK

Answer:

14. A box has 90 markers. If you want to divide them equally among 10 kids, how many markers will each kid get?

SHOW YOUR WORK

Answer:

15. If there are 25 toys and you want to divide them equally among 5 boxes, how many toys will be in each box?

SHOW YOUR WORK

Answer:

Time to grade yourself. To pass this mission, you need to answer at least 10 questions correctly. In the top section of the circle below, write how many you got correct.

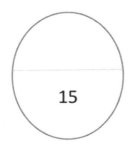

15

If you answered 10 or more correctly, then congratulations! You have earned the following badge:

Because of your efforts, Spooky will get a new pet.

But if you answered fewer than 10 correctly, don't worry! You can try again and still earn the badge and help Spooky.

Riddle: I am a word of letters three; add two and fewer there will be. What word am I?

Answer: Few.

Answers for Mission 9

1. 3
2. 6
3. 3
4. 5
5. 3
6. 4
7. 8
8. 4
9. 5
10. 3
11. 9
12. 7
13. 9
14. 9
15. 5

CHAPTER 9

Fractions

Introduction

Fractions are a very important part of mathematics. In this chapter, we will learn about fractions and their different parts.

A fraction is a part of a whole. For example, if you cut a pizza into eight pieces, each piece is a fraction of the whole pizza. Fractions are made up of two parts: the numerator and the denominator.

$$\underset{\text{(total parts in whole)}}{\underset{\text{denominator}}{5}} \quad \frac{\overset{\text{numerator (number of parts we have)}}{2}}{5}$$

The numerator is the top number of the fraction and represents how many parts we are talking about. The denominator is the bottom number of the fraction and represents the total number of equal parts in the whole.

If we have a pizza that is cut into eight equal slices,

and we take three slices, we can write this as the fraction 3/8. In this case, the numerator is 3, which represents the number of slices we took, and the denominator is 8, which represents the total number of slices in the pizza.

Let's look at few more examples:

1. The circle below is divided into 8 equal parts with 4 parts shaded. Here is how to write it as a fraction:

   Number of parts shaded = 4

   Total parts = 8

   As a fraction: 4/8.

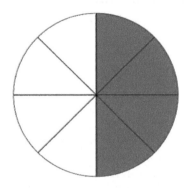

2. This time the circle is divided into 6 equal parts and 4 of them are shaded.

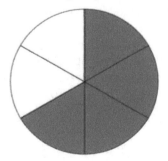

   Number of parts shaded = 4

   Total parts = 6

   As a fraction: 4/6.

3. Look at the circle below. It is divided into 3 equal parts with 2 parts shaded.

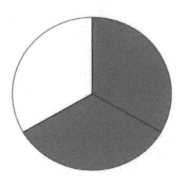

Number of parts shaded = 2

Total parts = 3

As a fraction: 2/3.

4. Look at the bar below and let us write the fraction for it.

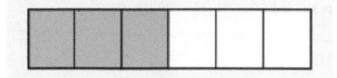

Number of parts shaded = 3

Total parts = 6

As a fraction: 3/6.

Spooky's Big Bossy Brother

Spooky has been doing great in class. His older brother, who is in 5th grade now, has been bragging a lot about how good he was in fractions when he was in 3rd grade. Big Brother has been telling Spooky how he cleared the division mission that their dad gave to him. Spooky is little bit annoyed by this and has decided to learn fractions on his own. His plan is to learn fractions and complete the mission without Big Brother knowing.

Spooky read the rules of the mission. According to the rules, there will be 15 fraction questions and if he can answer at least 10 of them correctly, the mission will be completed. Some questions in the mission may be challenging, so Spooky can build a team, make any kid the captain of his team. The team can help him clear the mission. Spooky believes there is no one better than you in fractions, so he wants you to be the captain of his team. Are you read to help Spooky? I hope you jumped in air and said "Yes!" Before you help, let's do some practice.

Practice Questions

Practice Questions

Let's do some more practice before we try to complete our next mission. Write the fractions shown:

1.

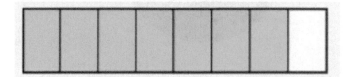

Answer: Number of parts shaded = 7

Total parts = 8

As a fraction: 7/8.

2.

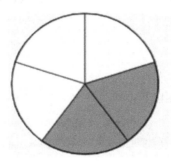

Answer: Number of parts shaded = 2

Total parts = 5

As a fraction: 2/5.

3.

Answer: Number of parts shaded = 1

Total parts = 6

As a fraction: 1/6.

4.

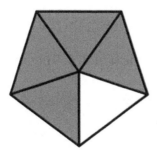

Answer: Number of parts shaded = 4

Total parts = 5

As a fraction: 4/5.

5.

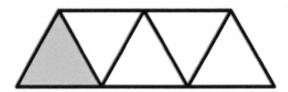

Answer: Number of parts shaded = 1

Total parts = 5

As a fraction: 1/5.

6. What fractions of the balls are white balls?

Answer: Number white balls = 3

Total balls = 8

As a fraction: 3/8.

7. Leah has 1 cat and 2 dogs. What fraction of Leah's pets are dogs?

Answer: Total pets = 3 (2 dogs and 1 cat)

Number of dogs = 2

Fraction of Leah's pets that are dogs = 2/3.

Number Lines:

Fractions can be shows on number lines also.

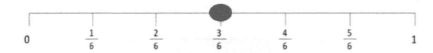

The red dot on the line above shows fraction 3/6. The line is divided into 6 equal parts and we have put marker on the 3rd part.

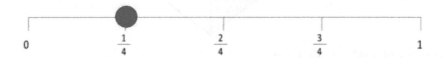

The line above shows fraction 1/4. The line is divided into 4 equal parts and we have put marker on the 1st part.

Understanding Equivalent Fractions

To understand equivalent fractions, let's look at the two circles below. The first circle is divided into 4 equal parts with 2 parts shaded. Therefore, the fraction is 2/4.

The second circle is divided into 8 equal parts with 4 parts shaded. So, the fraction is 4/8.

It is evident from the picture below that both circles have an equal shaded area. This means that 2/4 = 4/8. Therefore, 2/4 is an equivalent fraction of 4/8.

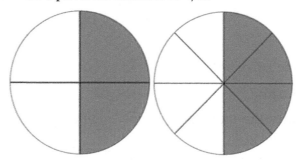

Equivalent fractions are fractions that have the same value but are written differently.

How to determine if two fractions are equivalent:

To find an equivalent fraction, we can multiply or divide both the numerator and the denominator by the same number. For example, to find an equivalent fraction for 2/3, we can multiply both the numerator and denominator by 2, which gives us 4/6. 4/6 is equivalent to 2/3 because they both represent the same value.

Fun Exercise: Let us say we are asked to find 6 equivalent fractions of 1/2. How can we do that?

Answer: To find equivalent fractions of 1/2 we can multiply the denominator and numerator by the same number. The numerator in ½ is 1 and the denominator is 2.

We can choose any number to multiply by, as long as we multiply both the numerator and the denominator by the same number.

Therefore, here are some equivalent fractions of 1/2:

    a)   1/2 x 2/2 = 2/4

    b)   1/2 x 3/3 = 3/6

    c)   1/2 x 4/4 = 4/8

    d)   1/2 x 5/5 = 5/10

    e)   1/2 x 7/7 = 7/14

    f)   1/2 x 11/11 = 11/22

There can be infinite number of equivalent fractions for a fraction.

How to determine if two fractions are equivalent

Question: Find if 3/4 and 6/8 are equivalent fractions?

Answer: There are two ways we can find out if these two fractions are equivalent.

Method 1:

Let's first examine the denominators in both fractions.

In the fraction 3/4, the denominator is 4. In the fraction 6/8, the denominator is 8. Our first goal is to find an equivalent fraction of ¾ with a denominator of 8, so that we can compare them with the same denominator.

We know that 4 x 2 = 8.

So, to find the equivalent fraction of ¾ we will multiply the numerator by 2 and the denominator by 2.

$$3/4 \times 2/2 = 6/8$$

So, 6/8 is an equivalent fraction of 3/4.

Method 2: Butterfly Method

In this method, we multiply the numerator of one number by the denominator of the other number. Numbers are 3/4 and 6/8

First, we multiply the numerator of the first fraction by the denominator of the second fraction

$$3 \times 8 = 24$$

Then, we multiply the numerator of the second fraction by the denominator of the first fraction.

$$6 \times 4 = 24.$$

If the result of both multiplications is the same, the two fractions are equivalent. In this case, the result of both the multiplications is 24, therefore the fractions are equivalent.

Practice Questions:

Practice Questions

1. Determine if the following fractions are equivalent: 2/3 and 4/6

    Answer: You can use either of the methods described above to determine if the fractions are equivalent. I am going to show using both methods.

Method:1

The denominator in the second fraction is 6. The denominator in the first fraction (2/3) is 3.

The first step for us is to find an equivalent fraction of 2/3 with a denominator of 6. We know that 3 x 2 =6.

So, we will multiply first fraction with 2/2.

2/3 x 2/2 = 4/6

Therefore, 4/6 is an equivalent fraction of 2/3.

Method:2 Using Butterfly method

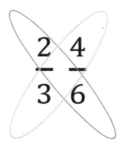

First, we multiply the numerator of the first fraction by the denominator of the second fraction

2 x 6 = 12

Then, we multiply the numerator of the second fraction by the denominator of the first fraction.

4 x 3 = 12.

Since the result of both multiplications is the same, the two fractions are equivalent.

2.   Determine if the following fractions are equivalent: 2/3 and 10/12

Answer:

The denominator in the second fraction (10/12) is 12.

The denominator in first fraction (2/3) is 3.

First step is to find an equivalent fraction of 2/3 with a denominator of 12.

We know that 3 x 4 =12.

So, we will multiply the first fraction with 4/4.

2/3 x 4/4 = 8/12

So, 8/12 is an equivalent fraction of 2/3. We did not get 10/12 when we found an equivalent fraction of 2/3 with a denominator of 12. Therefore, 10/12 is not an equivalent fraction of 2/3.

Comparing Fractions

In this section, we will learn how to compare fractions.

Comparing Fractions with the Same Denominator

When you have two fractions with the same denominator, they have same number of total parts. You can compare the numerator to see which one is bigger.

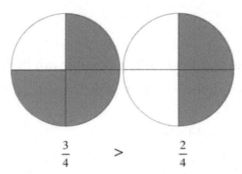

$$\frac{3}{4} \quad > \quad \frac{2}{4}$$

Both the shapes above are equal in size. The first shape is divided into 4 equal parts and 3 parts are shaded. So, the fraction is 3/4. The second shape is divided into 4 equal parts and 2 parts are shaded. So, the fraction is 2/4. The total number of parts (denominator) is same in both shapes. Since the first shape has a higher numerator, that means the first shape is shaded more.

So, 3/4 > 2/4.

Comparing Fractions with Different Denominators

As we have seen in the previous section, if we can make the denominator the same when comparing two fractions, then the fraction with larger numerator is greater than the fraction with smaller numerator. To compare two fractions with different denominators, we will try to find an equivalent fraction of the first fraction with the same denominator as the second fraction. Let us try to understand this with an example.

Let us say we have two fractions: 1/4 and 4/12. We need to find out which fraction is bigger.

First, look at the denominators of both fractions. They are not equal. The second fraction has a higher denominator. So, our first step is to find an equivalent fraction of 1/4 with a denominator of 12. How can 4 reach 12? We know that 4 x 3 = 12. Therefore, we will multiply the numerator and denominator of the first fraction by 3.

1/4 x 3/3 = 3/12

So, 3/12 is an equivalent fraction of 1/4.

Now we can easily compare 3/12 (equivalent to 1/4) and 4/12. Both fractions have the same denominator. Fraction 2 has a larger numerator, therefore 4/12 > 3/12. Since 3/12 = 1/4, this also means that 4/12 > 1/4.

Practice Questions

Compare each pair of fractions.

1. **1/3 and 2/3**

Answer: We will go step by step.

Step 1: Do these fractions have the same denominator?

Answer: Yes.

Step 2: If the denominators are the same, then the fraction with the larger numerator is greater than the fraction with the smaller numerator.

Therefore, 2/3 > 1/3.

2.   **1/4 and 3/8**

Answer: We will go step by step.

Step 1: Do these fractions have the same denominator?

Answer: No.

Step 2: If the denominators are not the same, we will first determine which fraction has the smaller denominator.

Answer: 1/4

Step 3: We will now try to find an equivalent fraction of 1/4 with a denominator of 8. How can we make 4 reach 8?

Answer: 4 x 2 = 8. That means we will multiply the numerator and denominator of first fraction (1/4) with 2.

Step 4: Find an equivalent fraction of 1/4 with a denominator of 8

Answer: 1/4 x 2/2 = 2/8

Step 5: Now compare the equivalent fraction we got in step 4 (2/8) with second fraction (3/8). Both fractions now have the same denominator. So, the fraction with the larger numerator wins.

2/8 < 3/8 or 1/4< 3/8

3.   **1/5 and 4/20**

Answer: Again, we will go step by step.

Step 1: Do these fractions have the same denominator?

Answer: No.

Step 2: If the denominators are not the same, we will first determine which fraction has the smaller denominator.

Answer: 1/5

Step 3: We will now try to find an equivalent fraction of 1/5 with a denominator of 20. How can 5 reach 20?

Answer: 5 x 4 = 20. That means we will multiply numerator and denominator of the first fraction (1/5) with 4.

Step 4: Find an equivalent fraction of 1/5

Answer: 1/5 x 4/4 = 4/20

Step 5: Now, we compare the equivalent fraction we obtained in step 4 (4/20) with the second fraction (4/20). Both fractions have the same denominator. So, the fraction with greater numerator wins. In this case, both fractions have the same numerator.

Therefore,

4/20 = 4/20 or 1/5 = 4/20

Adding and Subtracting Fractions

In this section, we will learn how to add and subtract fractions with the same denominator.

To add or subtract fractions with the same denominator, we simply add or subtract the numerators and keep the denominator the same. For example, to add 1/4 and 2/4, we add the numerators (1+2) and keep the denominator the same (4), which gives us 3/4.

Therefore

1/4 + 2/4 = 3/4

Similarly

3/4 - 2/4 = 1/4

Practice Questions

Add the following fractions:

1. 1/4 + 2/4

    Answer: Since the denominators are the same, we can simply just add the numerators.

    1/4 + 2/4 = 3/4

2. 3/5 + 2/5

    Answer:

    3/5 + 2/5 = 5/5

Subtract the following fractions:

3. 3/4 - 2/4

    Answer: Since the denominators are the same, we can simply subtract the numerators. Numerators are 3 and 2.

    3 - 2 = 1.

    Therefore, 3/4 - 2/4 =1/4.

4. 6/7 - 3/7

    Answer: Since the denominators are the same, just subtract the numerators.

    Numerators are 6 and 3. 6 - 3 = 3.

    Therefore, 6/7 - 3/7 = 3/7.

Mission 10

**Ready for
Mission**

It's time to help Spooky complete the mission. You need to answer at least 10 questions correctly to pass this mission. If you clear this mission, then Spooky will able to tell his bossy brother that he also knows fractions. Good luck!

Answer the following questions:

Note: For comparing the fractions, find out if the fractions are equivalent, or which fraction is greater than the other.

1. Write the fraction shown:

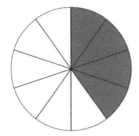

   Answer:

   Number of parts shaded = _____

   Total parts = _____

   As a fraction: _____

2. Write the fraction shown:

   Answer:

   Number of parts shaded = _____

   Total parts = _____

   As a fraction: _____

3. A pizza has 8 slices. If 3 of the slices have pepper, what fraction of the pizza slices have pepper?

   Answer:

   Number of slices with pepper = _____

   Total slices = _____

   As a fraction: _____

4. Ryan has 2 dogs and 2 cats. What fraction of Ryan's pets are dogs?

   Answer:

   Number of dog pets = _____

   Total number of pets = _____

   As a fraction: _____

5. Is this statement true or false: 4/8 is an equivalent fraction 2/4?

   Answer:

SHOW YOUR WORK

6. Compare the fractions: 7/8 and 3/8 and find out which fraction is greater?

   Answer:

SHOW YOUR WORK

7. Compare the fractions: 2/6 and 1/3 and find out if the two fractions are equivalent?

Answer:

SHOW YOUR WORK

8. Compare the fractions: 3/7 and 5/7 and find out which fraction is greater?

Answer:

SHOW YOUR WORK

9. Add the following fractions: 2/7 + 3/7.

Answer:

10. Emily ate 2/3 of a pizza and her brother ate 1/3 of the same pizza. What fraction of the pizza was eaten in total?

Answer:

SHOW YOUR WORK

11. Sally has 1/3 of a cup of sugar, and she wants to add 1/3 of a cup more to the mix. How much sugar will Sally have in total?

    Answer:

SHOW YOUR WORK

12. 3/4 is an equivalent fraction of 9/16. True or false?

    Answer:

SHOW YOUR WORK

13. 3/4 is an equivalent fraction of 9/12. True or false?

    Answer:

SHOW YOUR WORK

14. Write the fraction shown:

Answer:

Number of parts shaded = _____

Total parts = _____

As a fraction: _____

15. Write the fraction shown:

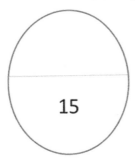

Answer:

Number of parts shaded = _____

Total parts = _____

As a fraction: _____

Time to grade yourself. To pass this mission, you need to answer at least 10 questions correctly. You can verify your answers, or you can ask someone in your family to check your work. In the top section of the circle below, write how many you got correct.

15

If you answered 10 or more correctly, then congratulations! You have earned the following badge:

Because of your efforts, Spooky can tell his bossy brother that he is as good as he is in fractions.

But if you answered less than 10 correctly, don't worry, you can try again and still earn the badge and help Spooky.

Riddle: Why are teddy bears never hungry?

Answer: Because they are always stuffed.

Answers for Mission 10

1. 4/10
2. 3/4
3. 3/8
4. 2/4
5. True
6. 7/8
7. Equivalent
8. 5/7 > 3/7
9. 5/7
10. 2/3 + 1/3 = 3/3
11. 2/3
12. False
13. True
14. 2/7
15. 4/5

CHAPTER 10

Time to the Minute

Introduction

In this chapter, we'll be learning about time. Time is something that we use every day, and it helps us to know when to do things like eat, sleep, and go to school.

First, we need to understand that time is measured in hours, minutes, and seconds. There are 60 seconds in one minute and 60 minutes in one hour. There are 24 hours in one day.

We use clocks to measure time. There are two types of clocks: analog clocks and digital clocks.

An analog clock has a face with two hands: a shorter hour hand and a longer minute hand. The minute hand on the clock moves around the clock face every hour, and it takes 60 minutes for it to complete a full circle.

To read an analog clock, we look at the position of the hands. The hour hand points to the hour and the minute hand points to the minute. We read the hour first, then the minute. For example, if the hour hand is pointing to the 8 and the minute hand is pointing to the 12, we say that it is 8:00.

A digital clock shows the time in numbers. To read a digital clock, we look at the numbers on the display. The first two numbers show the hour and the last two numbers show the minutes. For example, if the display shows 12:08, we say that it is 12:08.

How to determine minutes on analog clock. The picture below shows how to read minutes. If the long hand is on 1 that means 5 minutes. If the long hand is on 2 that means 10 minutes. As the long hand moves to the next number keep on adding 5. So, if it is at 6, then either add number 5 six times or do 5 x 6 = 30.

If the minute hand is between two numbers. For example, in the picture below, the long hand (minutes) is between 3 and 4. It is at three marks after the number 3. To determine minute, we will do 5 x 3 + 3 = 18 minutes.

Now, let's practice reading time on analog clocks. Look at the clock faces below

The hour clock is between 10 and 11. So, the hour is 10.

The long hand is on 4. So, the long hand shows 5 x 4 = 20 minutes past the hour. So, the time is 10:20.

Great job! Now you know how to read analog clocks. We will do some practice questions now.

Practice Questions

Practice Questions

1.   Write the time:

Answer: The short hand is between 3 and 4. So, the hour is 3.

The long hand is between 9 and 10. It is at three marks after the number 9. To determine minute, we will do 5 x 9 + 3 = 48 minutes.

So, the time is 3:48

2.   Write the time:

Answer: The short hand is between 6 and 7. So, the hour is 6.

The long hand is between 5 and 6. It is at one mark after the number 5. To determine minute, we will do 5 x 5 + 1= 26 minutes.

Therefore, the time is 6:26

Elapsed Time

Elapsed time is the amount of time that has passed between two events. We use elapsed time to calculate how long something has taken, like how long we've been at the park or how long we've been doing our homework.

To calculate elapsed time, we need to know the start time and the end time of the event. We can use a clock to help us figure out the time. We need to subtract the start time from the end time to find the elapsed time.

For example, if we start playing outside at 3:30 and we stop playing at 4:15, we can calculate the elapsed time by subtracting 3:30 from 4:15. It will be 45 minutes. From 3:30 to 4:00 it is 30 minutes, and from 4:00 to 4:15 it is 15 minutes. So, the total is 30 + 15 = 45 minutes.

Practice Questions

Practice Questions

1. Sofia started watching a movie at 8:00 pm. The movie ended at 10:15 pm. How long was the movie?

    Answer: We need to find the elapsed time between the starting time and ending time, which is the length of the movie.

    Movie started at 8 p.m.

    Movie ended at 10:15 p.m.

    So, from 8 p.m. to 9 p.m. is 1 hour. From 9 p.m. to 10 p.m. is 1 hour. And then from 10 p.m. to 10:15 p.m. is 15 minutes.

    Total movie time = 2 hours and 15 minutes.

2. Monica finished her homework at 5:45 pm. She played outside for 1 hour and 30 minutes. What time did she come back inside?

    Answer: To solve this problem, we need to add the amount of time Monica played outside to the time she finished her homework.

    We can start by converting the 1 hour and 30 minutes to minutes:

    1 hour and 30 minutes = 90 minutes

    Then, we can add the minutes to the time Monica finished her homework:

    5:45 pm + 90 minutes = 7:15 pm

    Therefore, Monica came back inside at 7:15 pm.

Mission 11

**Ready for
Mission**

It's time to help Spooky complete the mission. You need to answer at least 3 questions correctly to clear this mission. Good luck!

1. Mia woke up at 6:30 am. She brushed her teeth for 5 minutes, got dressed for 15 minutes, and had breakfast for 20 minutes. What time did she finish her breakfast?

    Answer:

SHOW YOUR WORK

2. Write the time:

    Answer:

3. Emily started reading a book at 7:00 pm and finished at 8:15 pm. How long did it take her to read the book?

    Answer:

SHOW YOUR WORK

4. A football game started at 1:30 pm and ended at 4:15 pm. How long was the game?

Answer:

SHOW YOUR WORK

5. Maria started her homework at 4:45 pm and finished at 6:00 pm. How long did it take her to finish her homework?

Answer:

SHOW YOUR WORK

Time to grade yourself. To pass this mission, you need to answer at least 3 question correctly. You can verify your answers, or you can ask someone in your family to check your work. In the top section of the circle below, write how many you got correct.

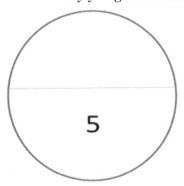

If you answered 3 or more correctly, then congratulations! You have earned the following badge:

But if you answered less than 3 correctly, don't worry, you can try again and still earn the badge.

Riddle: Which five-letter word gets shorter when two letters are added to it?

Answer: Short

Answers for Mission 11

1. 7:10 a.m.
2. 4:57
3. 1 hour and 15 minutes or 75 minutes
4. 2 hour and 45 minutes
5. 1 hour and 15 minutes

CHAPTER 11

Geometry

Introduction

In this chapter, we will learn about geometry, which is the study of shapes, sizes, and positions of objects. Geometry is all around us, from the shapes of buildings to the patterns on clothing. We are going to learn about 2D shapes, vertices, vertex, sides, parallel lines, and congruent sides.

Every 2D shape has two important parts: **sides** and **vertices**. The lines that form a 2D shape are called its **sides.**

A corner at which two sides of a 2D shape meet is called a **vertex.** Two or more corners are called **vertices.**

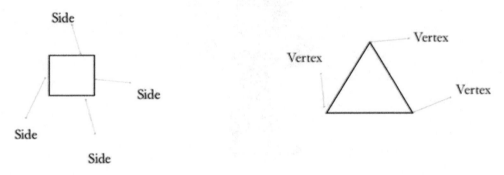

Rubiks Cube Classes

One of the fastest Rubik's cube solvers is in town and Spooky wants his mom to set up some classes with him so he can learn to solve a Rubik's cube. Mom wants Spooky to learn geometry first, and then complete a mission. If he completes the mission, then Mom will set up some classes for him. Mom told Spooky that some questions in the mission will be challenging, so Spooky can build a team, make any kid the captain of the team. Spooky thinks there is no one better than you in geometry, so he wants you to be the captain of his team.

Are you ready to help Spooky?

I hope you are pumped up and said "Yes!" Before we attempt to complete the mission, let's learn geometry.

Shapes:

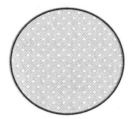

Circle: A 2D shape with no sides or vertices

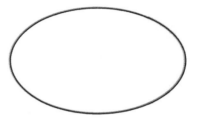

Oval: A stretched circle

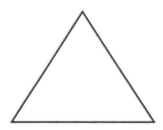

Triangle

A polygon with 3 sides and 3 vertices

Square

A polygon with 4 sides 4 vertices with all equal or congruent sides, 4 right angles and has 2 sets of parallel sides.

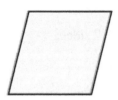

Parallelogram

A polygon with 4 sides, 4 vertices and 2 pairs of parallel sides

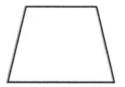

Trapezoid

A polygon with 4 sides, 4 vertices and 1 pair of parallel sides

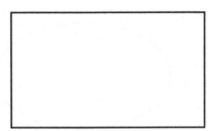

Rectangle

A polygon with

2 pairs of parallel sides, 4 sides,

4 vertices and 4 right angles

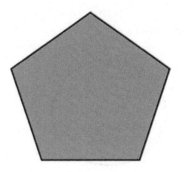

Pentagon

A polygon with 5 sides

and 5 vertices

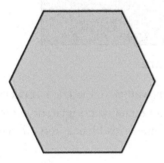

Hexagon

A polygon with 6 sides

And 6 vertices

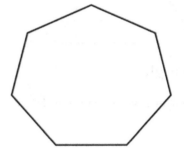

Heptagon

A polygon with 7 sides.

Octagon

A Polygon with 8 sides.

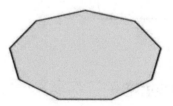

Nonagon

A Polygon with 9 sides.

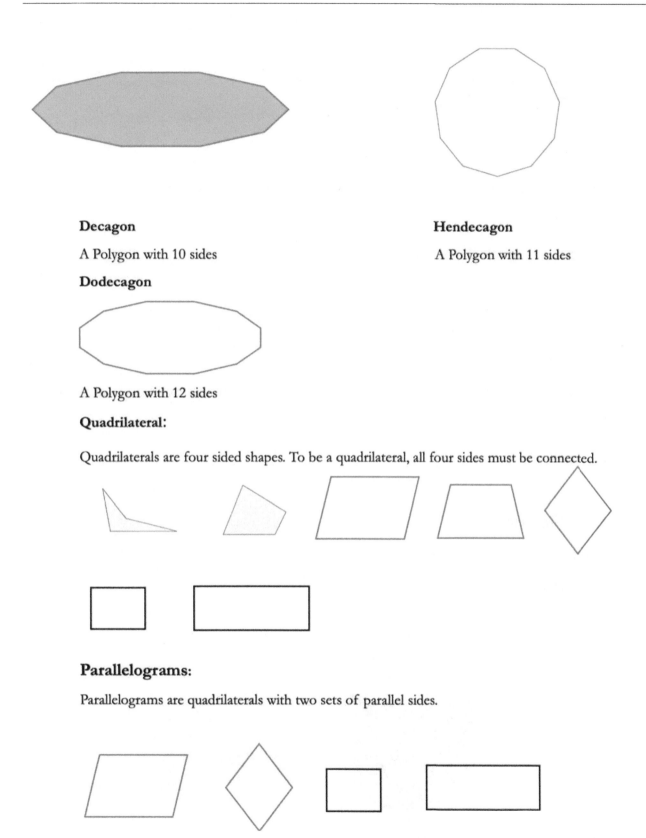

Decagon

A Polygon with 10 sides

Hendecagon

A Polygon with 11 sides

Dodecagon

A Polygon with 12 sides

Quadrilateral:

Quadrilaterals are four sided shapes. To be a quadrilateral, all four sides must be connected.

Parallelograms:

Parallelograms are quadrilaterals with two sets of parallel sides.

Rectangles:

Rectangles are parallelograms with 4 right angles.

Opposite sides of a rectangle are the same length (Congruent).

Rhombuses:

Rhombuses are parallelograms with four sides of equal length.

Squares:

A square is a rectangle with 4 equal sides. They are also rhombuses with four right angles.

Solid Figures:

Solid figures are three dimensional objects.

Some examples of Solid figures are

Cube:

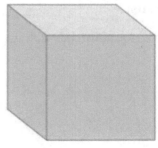

A Cube has 6 faces, 12 edges and 8 vertices.

Sphere:

A Sphere has 0 faces, 0 edge and 0 vertices.

Cone:

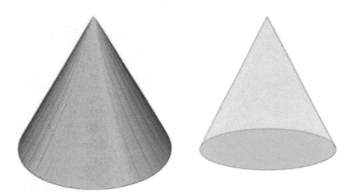

A cone has 1 face, 0 edge and 1 vertex.

Cylinder:

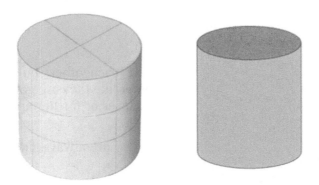

A cylinder has 2 faces, 0 edges and 0 vertices.

Rectangular Prism:

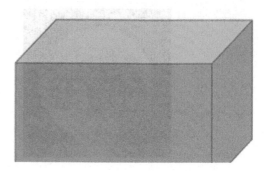

A rectangular prism has 6 faces, 12 edges and 8 vertices.

Square Pyramid:

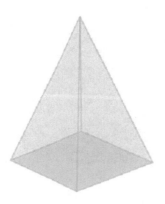
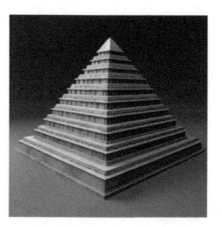

A square pyramid has 5 faces, 8 edges and 5 vertices.

Parallel lines:

Parallel lines are lines that never intersect or cross each other, no matter how far they are extended. When you draw parallel lines, they will look like they are going in the same direction, like two friends walking together but never getting closer or farther apart. They will always stay the same distance away from each other.

Remember, parallel lines never cross or intersect. They are always side by side and never meet. Look at the two parallel lines below.

Question: In what ways can the polygon below be classified?

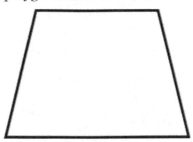

Answer: Quadrilateral, Trapezoid

Funny Joke: What did the egg say when she was late for breakfast?

Answer: I have got to scramble.

Mission 12

**Ready for
Mission**

It's time to help Spooky complete the mission. You need to answer at least 5 questions correctly to clear this mission. Good Luck.

1.   Draw a rectangle that is not square.

Draw here

2.   Write the name of the following shape:

Answer:

3.   Write the name of the following shape.

Answer:

4.   Draw a parallelogram that is not rhombus.

Draw here

5.   Draw a rhombus that is not a square.

Draw here

6.   Circle all the quadrilaterals in the table below:

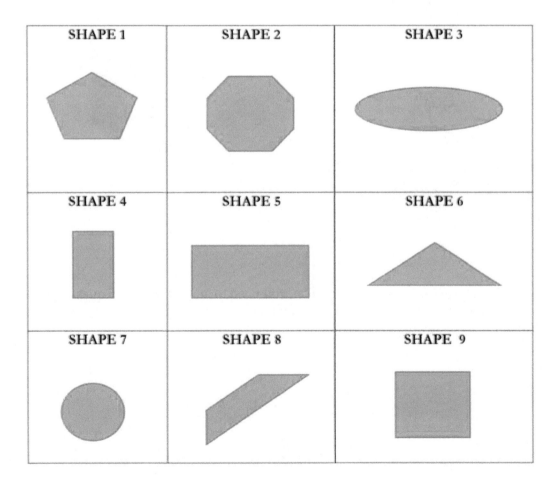

Answer:

7. Which 3D shape is this?

Answer:

8. Circle all the 3D shapes below:

Answer:

Time to grade yourself. To pass this mission, you need to answer at least 5 questions correctly. You can verify your answers, or you can ask someone in your family to check your work. In the top section of the circle below, write how many you got correct.

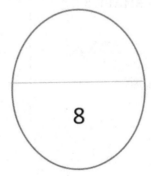

If you answered 5 or more correctly, then congratulations! You have earned the following badge:

But if you answered less than 5 correctly, don't worry, you can try again and still earn the badge.

Riddle: Which question can you never answer "yes" to?

Answer: "Are you asleep?"

Answers for Mission 12

1. Answer can vary - Make sure the rectangle you draw does not have all four sides equal.

2. Octagon

3. Pentagon

4. Answer can vary – Make sure the parallelogram you draw does not have all 4 sides equal.

5. Answer can vary -Rhombus and square both have all sides of equal length. Make sure the rhombus you draw does not have right angles.

6. Shapes: 4,5,8 and 9

7. Cylinder

8. Shapes: 3 and 5

CHAPTER 12

Counting Money

In this chapter, you will learn how to count different types of coins and bills to make different amounts of money.

Counting Coins: A Fun and Easy Way to Learn About Money

Let's start with coins. Coins come in different sizes, shapes, and values. In the United States, we use five different types of coins: penny, nickel, dime, quarter, and a half dollar.

The penny is worth one cent, the nickel is worth five cents, the dime is worth ten cents, the quarter is worth twenty-five cents, and the half dollar coin is worth 50 cents.

To count coins, you need to know the value of each coin and how many of each you have. For example, if you have two nickels and three dimes, you can add the value of each coin to find the total amount of money.

> 2 nickels = 2 x 5 cents = 10 cents
>
> 3 dimes = 3 x 10 cents = 30 cents
>
> Total = 10 cents + 30 cents = 40 cents

Counting Bills

In addition to coins, we also use bills to make purchases. Bills come in different denominations, or values, ranging from $1 to $100.

To count bills, you need to know the value of each bill and how many of each you have. For example, if you have two $5 bills and three $10 bills, you can add the value of each bill to find the total amount of money.

2 $5 bills = 2 x $5 = $10

3 $10 bills = 3 x $10 = $30

Total = $10 + $30 = $40

Counting Mixed Coins and Bills

Sometimes, you may have a combination of coins and bills. To count mixed coins and bills, you can follow the same steps as before.

For example, if you have one dime, two quarters, and two $5 bills, you can add the value of each coin and bill to find the total amount of money.

> 1 dime = 10 cents
>
> 2 quarters = 2 x 25 cents = 50 cents
>
> 2 $5 bills = 2 x $5 = $10
>
> Total = 10 cents + 50 cents + $10 = $10.60

Making Change

One important skill in counting money is making change. When you make a purchase, you may need to give the cashier more money than the cost of the item. The cashier will then give you change back.

To make change, you can subtract the cost of the item from the amount of money you gave the cashier. For example, if you buy a toy for $4 and give the cashier a $10 bill, you can subtract $4 from $10 to find the change.

> $10 - $4 = $6

The cashier should give you $6 in change, which may include coins and bills.

A Trip to the Zoo

Megan and Spooky want to go to the zoo. They have $10 combined. The zoo ticket is $20 each. So, they need $40. Spooky asks his dad for $30. His dad said, "Yes", but only on one condition. He has to complete a math mission on counting money. Dad said, "Some questions in the mission will be challenging, so Spooky and Megan can build a team, make any kid the captain of the team." Spooky thinks there is no one better than you in counting money, so he wants you to be the captain of his team.

Are you ready to be the captain of Spooky's team and help Spooky?

I hope you are excited and said, "Yes."

Let's do some practice before we try to complete the mission.

Practice Questions:

Practice Questions

1. Arjun had 35 dollars. His grandfather gave him $20 for his birthday. How much money does Arjun has now?

    Answer: Arjun now has $35 + $20 = $55.

2. Aaron has three $20 bills. He buys a toy for 31 dollars. How much money is he left with?

    Answer: Total money Aaron has = 3 x 20 = $60

    Amount of money he spends on toy: $31

    So, Aaron is left with $60 – $31 = $29.

3. Jose has 2 quarters, 4 dimes, and 3 nickels, how much money does he have in total?

    Answer: Total money Jose has = (2 x 25) + (4 x 10) + (3 x 5)= 50 + 40+ 15 = 105 cents. Note: 105 cents = 1 dollar bill and one nickel

4. If you buy a toy for $8 and give the cashier a $10 bill, how much change should you receive?

    Answer: You will get back $10 - $8 = $2

5. How much money is there? Count the Coins:

    Answer: Here we have 2 quarters, 1 dime, 2 nickels, 3 pennies and 1 half dollar coin.

    Total = (2 x 25) + (1 x 10) + (2 x 5) + (3 x 1) + (1 x 50) = 123 cents or $ 1.23.

Mission 13

Ready for Mission

It's time to help Megan and Spooky. You need to answer at least 5 questions correctly to complete this mission. Good luck!

1. If you have 4 nickels and 6 pennies, how much money do you have?

SHOW YOUR WORK

Answer:

2. If you have a 1 dollar bill, 2 quarters, and 3 dimes, how much money do you have?

SHOW YOUR WORK

Answer:

3. If you buy a candy bar for $0.75 and give the cashier a dollar bill, how much change will you receive?

SHOW YOUR WORK

Answer:

4. If you buy a toy for $2.50 and give the cashier a $5 bill, how much change will you receive?

SHOW YOUR WORK

Answer:

5. If you buy three erasers for $0.25 each, how much money do you need to pay the cashier?

SHOW YOUR WORK

Answer:

6. If you buy a piggy bank that costs $2.50 and give the cashier a $20 bill, how much change will you receive?

SHOW YOUR WORK

Answer:

7. If you buy a shirt that costs $7.99 and give the cashier a $20 bill, how much change will you receive?

SHOW YOUR WORK

Answer:

8.   If you buy a pack of gum that costs $0.75 and a candy bar that costs $1.50, how much money will you need to pay in total?

SHOW YOUR WORK

Answer:

Time to grade yourself. To complete this mission, you need to answer at least 5 question correctly. You can verify your answers, or you can ask someone in your family to check your work. In the top section of the circle below, write how many you got correct.

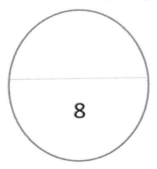

If you answered 5 or more correctly, then congratulations! You have earned the following badge:

But if you answered less than 5 correctly, don't worry! You can try again and still earn the badge and help Spooky.

Riddle: What is always in front of you but can't be seen??

Answer: The Future

Answers for Mission 13

1. 26 cents
2. 180 cents or $1.80
3. $0.25
4. $2.50
5. $0.75
6. $17.50
7. $12.01
8. $2.25

CHAPTER 13

Measurement

Introduction

In this chapter, we will learn about measurement and learn how to use different units to measure length, weight, and capacity.

Length:

Length is a measurement that tells us how long or short an object is. We use units like inches, feet, centimeters, and meters to measure length. We can use a ruler or measuring tape to measure the length of objects.

Let's look at an example: The length of the line in the picture shown below is 10 inches.

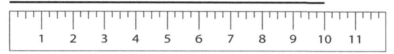

Let's do some practice:

1.

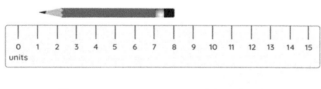

_ _ _ _ units.

Write the length of the pencil.

Answer: 7 units (Note that the distance is from 1 to 8)

2.   Length of a dolphin

Which unit can be used to measure the length of dolphin?

a)   Inches

b)   Feet

Answer: Feet

Weight:

Weight is another important measurement that tells us how heavy or light an object is. We use units like ounces, pounds, grams, kilograms, and tons to measure weight. We can measure weight using scales.

Examples of weights:

1. An apple weights about 6-7 ounces

2. A larger paper clip can weigh about 1 gram

3. A pineapple fruit has an average weight of about 1kg.

4. The average weight of a refrigerator is 250 pounds.

5. Weight of an elephant can be measured in tons

Based on the above information, think what's the closet estimate to weigh the following:

1. 1 crayon
   a) 8 grams
   b) 800 grams
   c) 4 kilograms
   Answer: 8 grams

2. A laptop
   a) 2 grams
   b) 200 grams
   c) 2 kilograms
   Answer: 2 kilograms

3. An airplane
   a) Kg
   b) Tons
   c) Grams
   Answer: Tons

Capacity:

Capacity refers to the amount of liquid or other substances that a container can hold. To measure capacity accurately, we use standard units.

Fluid Ounces (fl oz): Used for measuring smaller quantities of liquid. For example, the capacity of a small bottle of soda might be measured in fluid ounces.

Coca-Cola - 20 fl oz
Bottle

Cups, Pints, Quarts, and Gallons: Used for measuring larger quantities of liquid. For example, the capacity of a cooking pot or a milk container might be measured in cups, pints, quarts, or gallons.

1 Gallon (128 oz.)

Milliliters (ml): Used for measuring smaller quantities of liquid. For example, the capacity of a medicine bottle or a small container might be measured in milliliters.

Liters (l): Used for measuring larger quantities of liquid. For example, the capacity of a water jug or a milk carton might be measured in liters.

Based on the above information, determine what capacity unit can used for following:

1. Nail Paint

   a) 15 milliliters
   b) 15 liters
   c) 150 liters

   Answer: 15 milliliters

2. A bathtub

a) 3 liters

b) 300 milliliters

c) 300 liters

Answer: 300 liters.

Mission Impossible

Optional Mission: The questions in this mission are challenging. Feel free to attempt them if you would like to challenge yourself.

1) Find the missing number in:

   a) $(72 \div 9) = (? \div 8)$

2) Fill in the box with either >, < or = symbol:

   a) $72 + 217 \boxed{?} 25 \times 9$

3) The product of a one-digit number with itself is same as sum of the digit with itself. Which of the following could be that number?

   a) 3 b) 1 c) 2 d) 4

4) Which of the following would be the perimeter of an octagon with side 4 cm?

   a) 16cm b) 32cm c) 64cm d) 8cm

5) Which of the following pairs of numbers are odd?

   a) 70,81 b) 32, 55 c) 67, 55 d) 81,550

6) Which of the following numbers is not divisible by 5?

   a) 705 b) 165 c) 550 d) 542

7) Which of the following numbers is not divisible b 3?

   a) 714 b) 135 c) 1239 d) 608

8) A train departs from Station A at 10 p.m and reaches station B at 5 a.m the next day. What is the total time taken by the train to reach from A to B?

   a) 5 hrs b) 6 hrs c) 7 hrs d) 3 hrs

9) A polygon with seven sides is called:

   a) Hexagon b) Pentagon c) Heptagon d) Rectangle

10) What would be the next number in the following series of numbers: 8, 11, 14, 17,?

   a) 22 b) 21 c) 20 d) 44

11) A shopkeeper has 600 red apples and 200 green apples. On a particular day, he sells 200 red apples and 100 green apples. What is the fraction of apples sold to the total number of apples?

   a) 1/4 b) 1/3 c) 3/8 d) 5/8

12) A rectangular lawn of length 20m has an area of 200 square meters. Find the perimeter of the lawn

   a) 40m b) 30m c) 60m d) 60m

13) Choose the value of A, B, C, D in the following addition of two numbers

A31B

+ 2CD9

7156

    a) 4,6,28 b) 4,7, 8, 3 c) 4,5,28 d) 5,5,3,8

14) If

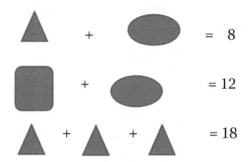

Find the value of   ?

    a) 4 b) 6 c) 12 d) 10

Answers:

1) 64
2) <
3) C
4) B
5) C
6) D
7) D
8) C
9) C
10) C
11) C
12) C
13) B
14) D

BONUS PRACTICE TEST

It's time to practice what we learned in the book. There are 30 questions on the test. Good Luck.

You can write your answers on a piece of paper and compare them with the answers provided at the end of this test.

1. Sarah has 15 pencils. She buys 10 more pencils from the store. How many pencils does Sarah have in total?

2. A school has 315 students in total. There are 127 boys in the school. How many girls are there in the school?

3. Three friends divided three pizzas into pieces. The shaded parts of the models represent the pieces that the friends ate.

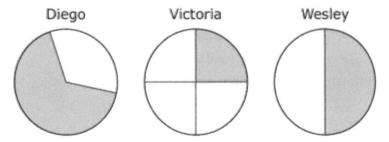

Which statement describes the fraction of a pizza that one of the friends ate?

a) Diego ate ½ of a pizza because he ate the largest piece of his 2 pieces.

b) Victoria ate 1/3 of a pizza, because she ate 1 piece and had 3 equal-size pieces left over.

c) Wesley ate ½ of a pizza because he ate 1 piece of his 2 equal-size pieces

4. The perimeter of a square is 40 cm. What is the length of each side?

5. What is 726 - 325?

	Hundreds	Tens	Ones
Borrow			
	7	2	6
-	3	2	5
Answer:			

6. A theater sold tickets for three movies. The table shows the number of tickets sold for each movie.

Movie	1	2	3
Number of Tickets	143	158	175

What was the total number of tickets the theater sold for these three movies?

A) 476

B) 366

C) 376

D) 473

7. Find the area of a rectangle that has length of 5 cm and width of 6 cm?

8. The side lengths of a rectangular mirror are shown in inches.

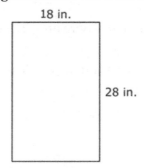

18 in.

28 in.

What is the perimeter of the mirror in inches?

A) 72 in.

B) 46 in.

C) 74 in.

D) 92 in.

9. Find out if this statement is true or false: Is 3/9 an equivalent fraction of 1/3?

10. There are 15 students in each classroom. If there are 3 classrooms, how many total students are there?

11. There are 32 flowers and you want to put them into 8 vases equally. How many flowers will be in each vase?

12. Arjun started his homework at 4:55 pm and finished at 6:45 pm. How long did it take him to finish his homework?

13. Add the following fractions: 3/7 + 3/7

14. Write the fractions shown:

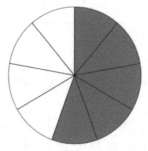

15. The table shows the numbers of baseball cards in different numbers of packages. Baseball Cards

Number of Packages	Number of Baseball Cards
2	22
3	33
4	44
5	55

Based on the relationship shown in the table, which statement is true¡

a) The number of packages times 1 equals the number of baseball cards.

b) The number of packages plus 1 equals the number of baseball cards.

c) The number of packages plus 11 equals the number of baseball cards.

d) The number of packages times 11 equals the number of baseball cards

16. Irene has a group of counters, as shown.

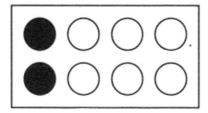

Which two fractions can represent the black counters in the group?

a) 2/6 and 2/8

b) 3/4 and 5/8

c) 2/8 and 1/4

17. Hector played a game 14 times. Each time he played, he threw 4 red balls and 3 green balls at a target. What was the total number of balls Hector threw at the target?

a) 21

b) 68

c) 98

d) 46

18. What is 14 x 10 equals to?

19. Is the number 4544444546789 even or odd?

20. There are 42 cupcakes and 6 friends want to share them equally, how many cupcakes will each friend get?

21. If you have 24 pencils and you want to put them in 4 equal groups, how many pencils will be in each group?

22. A box contains 6 apples. If there are 8 boxes, how many apples are there in total?

23. A rectangle is divided into 8 equal parts. John shaded 3 of the parts. What fraction of the rectangle did he shade?

24. Which comparison is NOT true?

   a)   17,090 > 2,984

   b)   34,162 < 3,986

   c)   16,538 > 15,981

   d)   2,438 < 3,438

25. On Saturday afternoon Marcus went to a swimming pool. The clock shows the time he arrived at the pool.

He left the pool 45 minutes later. At what time did Marcus leave the pool?

   a)   2:20 P.M.

   b)   7:55 P.M.

   c)   2:15 P.M.

   d)   3:20 P.M.

26. The perimeter of the rectangular floor of Mr. James cabin is 46 feet. The width of the floor is 10 feet. What is the length of the floor?

27. Find the difference: 10/11 - 9/11.

28. Gloria used the rule "subtract four" to make a number pattern. Which pattern could be Gloria's number pattern?

a) 24, 20, 16, 12

b) 17, 14, 11, 8

c) 19, 14, 9, 4

d) 31, 29, 27, 25

29. Which is equal to 3571?

    a) 300 + 500 + 700 + 100

    b) 300 + 50 + 71

    c) 3000 + 500 + 70 + 1

    d) 3000 + 57 + 1

30. Thomas has 152 baseball cards. His friend Mark has 129 baseball cards. How many more baseball cards does Thomas have than Mark?

    a) 23

    b) 37

    c) 271

    d) 281

Answers for Practice Test

1. 25 (15 + 10 = 25)
2. 188 (315 − 127 = 188)
3. C
4. 10 cm
5. 401
6. A (143 + 158 + 175 = 476)
7. 30 cm². (5 x 6 = 30)
8. D
9. True
10. 45 (15 x 3 = 45)
11. 4 (32 divided by 8 = 4)
12. 1 hour and 50 minutes
13. 6/7
14. 5/9
15. D

16. C
17. C
18. 140
19. Odd
20. 7 (42 divided by 6 = 7)
21. 6 (24 divided by 4 = 6)
22. 48 (6 x 8 = 48)
23. 3/8
24. B
25. A
26. 13 Feet
27. 1/11
28. A
29. C
30. A

FOR AMBITIOUS STUDENTS:

Welcome, ambitious learners! This special section is designed just for you. In these pages you will find challenges that go beyond the regular lessons. These activities are designed to encourage critical thinking. Ready for the challenge? Let the ambitious adventure begin!

1) Find the difference between the greatest three-digit number and the smallest three-digit number.

2) What number must be added to 4569 to get 7321?

3) A student reads a book from page 20 to page 51. How many pages did he read?

4) Find the number by adding the place value of 6 in the following four numbers

   a) 6120 b) 1620 c)1062 4) 1026

5) Henry has $250 in his account. He bought 5 books at $9 each. He also purchased 14 pens, with each pen costing $2. How much money is left with him?

6) Find the missing value (20 + 89) + 178 = 168 + ?

7) Find the number whose clue is below digits at various place value: 9 Thousand, 3 Hundred, 2 Tens 4 Ones.

8) The sum of Skyler and Ryan's ages is 18 years. What will be the sum of their ages after 4 years?

9) $171 needs to be distributed among 9 students. How much money will each student get?

10) The sides of a rectangle are 10m and 12 m. Ann walks 22m in 5 minutes. How much time will Ann take to walk around the rectangle?

11) Find the greatest number than can be formed by the digits 3,9,8,7.

12) Find the smallest number than can be formed by the digits 3,9,8,7.

13) A man spends money for 5 days. On the first day, he spends $1. After that, he spends thrice the money he spent the day before. How much money has he spent in 5 days?

14) Is the number 66789 divisible by 9?

15) Is it possible that a number is divisible by 6, but not by 3?

16) Look at the following figures:

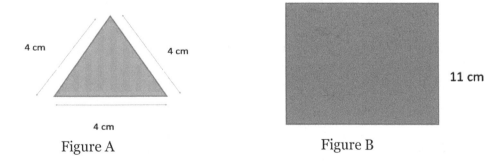

Figure A   Figure B

What is the fraction of the perimeter of figure A to the perimeter of figure B?

17) Which of the following numbers are odd numbers?

   a) 10 b) 36 c) 148 d) 171

18) Peter has 18 pens; his sister Anna has twice the number of pens as Peter. John, who is the brother of Peter has one–third of the number of pens Anna has. What is the total number of pens they have in total?

19) Round 8938 to the nearest hundred.

20) Henry scored 15 points more than Peter, who scored 60 points. Jack scored 20 more points than Henry. How many points did Jack score?

21) Round 71,450 to the nearest thousand.

22) Find the number of minutes in 20 hours?

23) Is the number 5444455 divisible by 5?

24) Find the missing number in the series: 1,5,10,15, 20, ?

25) Paul started exercising at 8:20 am and finished at 9:10 a.m. How long did he exercise?

26) The temperature of hot water is 15 degrees higher than the temperature shown below. What is the temperature of hot water?

27) A garden has a perimeter of 1600 m. One of its sides is 200m. Find the length of the other side?

28) Peter bought 8 apples, each costing 20 cents, 12 bananas each costing 5 cents, and 18 mangoes each costing 25 cents. What is the total cost?

29) How many sides does a Heptagon have?

30) How many pairs of parallel lines are there in a trapezoid?

Answers:

1) 999 – 100 = 899.

2) 7321-4569 = 2752

3) tricky question. 51 – 20 + 1 = 32. Remember to include 51st page.

4) 6666

5) $177

6) 119

7) 9324

8) 26

9) $19

10) 10 minutes

11) 9873

12) 3789

13) $121

14) Yes, sum of digits = 36, which is divisible by 9.

15) No

16) 12/44, which is equivalent to 3/11.

17) 171

18) 66

19) 8900

20) 95 points

21) 71,000

22) 1200 minutes

23) Yes, because the last digit is 5.

24) 25

25) 50 minutes

26) 55 degrees

27) 600 meters

28) $6.70

29) 7

30) One Pair

THANK YOU

Thank you for reading my book. If you have any questions or suggestions related to book, feel free to email me at 3rdGradeMathAdventures@gmail.com .

After reading this book, if you would like to schedule a personal online math coaching session for students up to 5th grade, I would be thrilled to help you master the wonderful world of math! Please feel free to email me at 3rdGradeMathAdventures@gmail.com to schedule a personalized 1:1 math coaching session. I am eager to assist you in your math journey! If you enjoy reading our book, kindly consider leaving a review for us on Amazon.

First and foremost, I want to express my heartfelt gratitude to my parents, both of whom are retired professors. Their guidance, wisdom, and vast knowledge in the field of education have been instrumental in shaping this book. Their dedication to learning and teaching have always been a source of inspiration for me, and I am honored to have inherited their passion for education.

To my beloved wife, who has been my rock throughout this entire journey, thank you for your unwavering support and encouragement. Your belief in me and this project kept me motivated even during the most challenging times.

I would like to express my deepest appreciation and gratitude to my son, Ryan Uppal, for his invaluable contributions to the development of this book. His expertise, keen eye for detail, and insightful suggestions have significantly enhanced the quality and clarity of the content.

Finally, to all the young readers and their parents who will embark on this mathematical journey with "3rd Grade Math Adventures," thank you for giving my book a chance to be a part of your lives. I hope it sparks curiosity, ignites a love for learning, and inspires the mathematicians and problem solvers of tomorrow.

With immense gratitude,

Amit Uppal

Author, "3rd Grade Math Adventures"

BADGES

1. ☐

2. ☐

3. ☐

4. ☐

5. ☐

6. ☐

7. ☐

8. ☐

9. ☐

10. ☐

11. ☐

12. ☐

13. ☐

Made in United States
Orlando, FL
16 December 2024

55992996R10091